By **MARGUERITE ICKIS**

WEAVING

as a hobby

1974

LITTLEFIELD, ADAMS & CO.

Totowa, New Jersey

Published 1974 by

LITTLEFIELD, ADAMS & CO.

by arrangement with Sterling Publishing Co., Inc.

Copyright © 1968 by Sterling Publishing Co., Inc.

Library of Congress Cataloging in Publication Data

Ickis, Marguerite, 1897–
  Weaving as a Hobby

  (A Littlefield, Adams Quality Paperback No. 287)
  SUMMARY: An introduction to weaving as a hobby,
including choosing and dressing a loom and suggestions
for patterns on two- and four-harness looms.
  Reprint of the ed. published by Sterling Pub. Co., New
York, in series: Sterling crafts books.

  1. Hand weaving.   [1. Hand weaving.   2. Weaving]
I. Title.

[TT848.I25 1974]   746.1'4   74-11262
ISBN 0-8226-0287-3

ACKNOWLEDGMENTS

The author and publisher wish to thank the following people and organizations for their assistance: Lily Mills, Shelby, North Carolina; Helen Slason of Countrywide Handweavers, Mission, Kansas; Martha Lehmann, New York City.

Color photos from "Small Webs" by courtesy of the copyright owner, ICA-Forlaget Aktiebolag, Vasteras, Sweden.

CONTENTS

Color plates opposite pages 32 and 64.

Illus. 1. Four-harness loom.

I. Beginning to Weave

Weaving, reduced to fundamentals, is a process of interlacing threads to form cloth. After forming a foundation of taut threads called the *warp*, the weaver goes over and under the warp threads at right angles with threads known as the *weft*. Designs are formed by varying the patterns of interlacing warp and weft threads, and by using different colors and materials.

This basic principle applies to all looms, no matter how complicated they might seem to you at first. Before long you will realize how simple the process of weaving actually is, even though it is one of the world's most intriguing crafts.

The best loom for a beginner is the versatile square weaver, which is easy to make and use. On it you will be able to make any number of things such as scarves, baby blankets, and even handbags, while you learn to produce patterns comparable to ones woven on a four-harness loom.

THE SQUARE WEAVER

This loom is designed for weaving 4″ squares which you can sew together later on to form almost any yarn article. Although you can make larger square looms, this size is preferable, since with it you will be able to use a 5″ or 6″ needle which will pick up the warp threads all the way across the loom in one simple operation.

Constructing the Loom

To make the loom, cut four pieces of soft wood such as pine or bass $\frac{1}{2}″ \times \frac{1}{2}″ \times 5″$ long, and mitre (dovetail) the corners. Glue the pieces together, and reinforce each corner with a small nail if the loom does not seem sturdy enough. To form the top of the loom upon

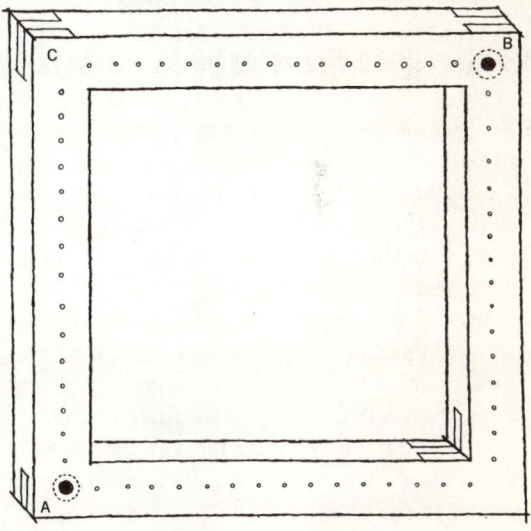

Illus. 2. The square weaver.

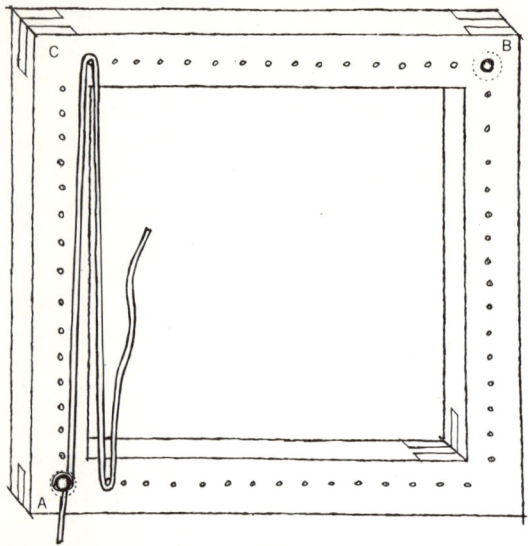

Illus. 3. The square weaver with the first row of warp.

Now set your nails on each dot and drive them in at least $\frac{1}{4}''$ deep, so they will provide a firm frame for weaving. When all the nails are in place your square weaver is ready for the warp.

Stringing the Warp

For this you will need a ball of 4-ply or medium-thick wool yarn in the color you have selected for your square. If this is your first attempt at weaving, a solid color dark square will give better results, since it will appear to stay cleaner. Later on you will learn how to make patterns on the square weaver, using this same method.

Place your loom in front of you so that corner A is near your left hand. Tie the yarn one inch from the end on to the nail in corner A, and begin to string the warp (Illus. 3) by carrying the yarn inside the line of nails to your left, up round the first nail near the upper left-hand corner of the loom (C), back down to the nail next to where you began, back up again, and so on until you reach the upper right-hand corner (B) of the loom. This completes the warp. While you are stringing, *try to maintain an even tension*, since the warp is the foundation of the final woven square.

The Weft

To measure the amount of yarn you will need for the weft, wind it round the outside of the nails on your loom eight times, and cut it off. This will leave you with plenty of yarn to spare. If the square is to be woven in two colors and you have the loom strung with the background color, tie on the weft or pattern thread at this point and measure the length in the same way. Thread your 5″ needle with the yarn. Now, starting at corner B, weave from right to left by passing the needle over the first

which you will wind the warp (Illus. 3), you will need 16 $\frac{3}{4}''$ headless or casing nails for each side of the loom. If headless nails are not available, buy 1″ nails and cut off the heads with a wire clipper.

The first step is to mark dots along each of the four 5″ sides of the loom, starting $\frac{1}{4}''$ from the inner edge of the lower left-hand corner (A). To ensure that your woven squares will be straight, before you drive the nails in, draw a guideline in the middle of each side of the loom. Measure your dots against this guideline to be sure they line up in a straight row in all directions.

Illus. 2 is a diagram showing how the nails are set. First, drive in one nail in each of two corners A and B which are diagonally across from each other. Then add fifteen nails $\frac{1}{4}''$ apart along the four sides. The two corner nails will give you a count of 16 nails in each row as shown in the illustration.

warp thread, under the next warp thread, and so on, across all 31 threads. You will bring the needle out over the warp thread just above corner A. Pull the yarn through gently, and loop it round the nail above A before you begin the next row.

The second row must be woven opposite to the first. To do this, you must go *under* all the threads you went *over* in the first row, and *over* those you went *under*. Since you went over the last thread in row 1, start row 2 by going under the first thread, over the second, and so on, across the row from left to right. The third row should be woven just like the first row, the fourth like row 2, etc. Thus every *other* row will be alike. Continue weaving back and forth across the loom until there is a loop round each nail in the loom. Your square will be complete when you bring the thread out beside the nail in corner A.

While you are weaving the weft, be very careful not to pull the yarn too tight or your square will be uneven. By passing the needle over the warp at a sharp angle (Illus. 4) each time you weave a row, and then easing the yarn into place gently with your needle, you will be able to control the tension at all times, and avoid unevenness.

After cutting off some of the excess weft thread, carefully push the square off the nails, and weave the two left-over ends into the edge of the square. At corner B you will find an extra loop of yarn left. Draw this in along the two woven edges and you will have a perfect square with fifteen loops on all four sides. These loops at the edges of the woven square will be matched with those of the next squares you make.

Sew your squares together with a darning needle and yarn to form scarves, a baby blanket,

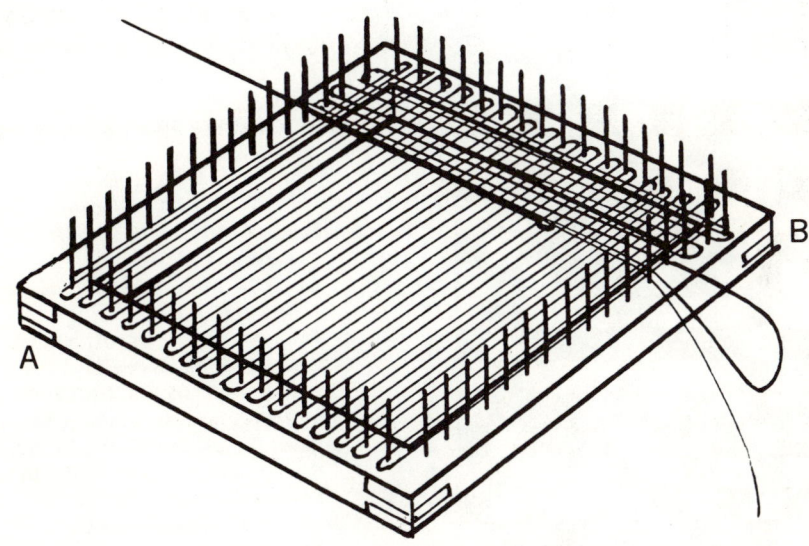

Illus. 4. How to weave the weft.

or anything you like. Block the finished article by covering it with a damp cloth and pressing lightly with a warm, not hot, iron.

As soon as you have mastered the one-color square, you are ready to go on to the next step: designing and weaving your own patterns.

PATTERN WEAVING

In most pattern weaving, the loom is first strung with warp threads, and then the pattern is woven in with weft threads carried on a needle.

There are many interesting weaving materials on the market, but for small looms such as the square weaver, it is important to use only those materials which have elasticity. If you do not string your loom with a thread that will "give," the warp threads may become too taut before you finish weaving. Four-ply wool yarn gives the most satisfactory results on a square weaver, but you may want to experiment with other materials when you have more experience.

If you weave the weft over and under, as you did in the first project, in a color which contrasts with the color of the warp threads, the result will be a plain or *tabby* weave. This produces a tweedlike effect.

By varying the over one and under one weave, however, you can achieve a multitude of patterns with the same two contrasting colors. To do this, you skip over or under two or more warp threads with the weft occasionally. Although this can be done at random, it is so simple to block out your own weaving designs in advance that random weaving is not recommended.

Planning a Design

To plan a design, take a piece of graph paper and block off as many squares as you have warp ends on each side of your loom. For example, your square weaver has 16 nails on each side, so make a graph 31 squares wide and 31 squares long. Each square represents what will show when the woven cloth is right side up. If the weft is passed under the warp the warp will

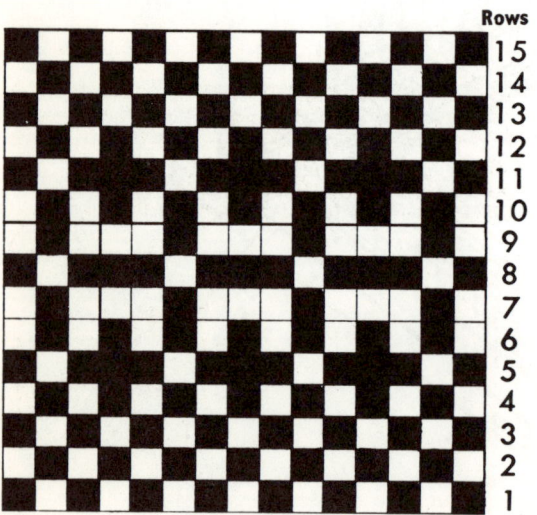

Rows
15
14
13
12
11
10
9
8
7
6
5
4
3
2
1

Illus. 5. A simple plain weave pattern.
Directions:

O = Over

U = Under

Row #1—U1, O1, U1, O1, U1, O1, etc. (plain weave).

Row #2—O1, U1, O1, U1, etc. (plain weave) (left to right).

Row #3—U1, O1, U1, O1, etc. (plain weave).

Row #4—Same as row 2.

Row #5—U1, O1, U3, O1, U3, O1, U3, O1, U1.

Row #6—Same as row 2.

Row #7—O1, U1, O3, U1, O3, U1, O3, U1, O1.

Row #8—U1, O1, U3, O1, U3, O1, U3, O1, U1.

Row #9—Same as row 7.

Row #10—Same as row 2.

Row #11—Same as row 5.

Row #12-15—Same as rows 1-3.

Illus. 6. Planning small squares.
Directions:
Row #1—Plain weave from right to left—
O, U, O, U, etc.
Row #2—From left to right—U, O, U3, O,
U, O, U, O, U3, O, U.
Row #3—O, U2, O, U2, O, U, O, U2, O, U2, O.
Row #4—U2, O, U, O, U2, O, U2, O, U, O, U2.
Row #5—U, O, U, O, U, O, U3, O, U, O, U, O,
U.
Row #6—Same as row 4.
Row #7—Same as row 3.
Row #8—Same as row 2.
Repeat rows 3 to 8 inclusive.
Last row #15—Plain weave, U, O, U, O, etc.

Weft thread
Warp thread

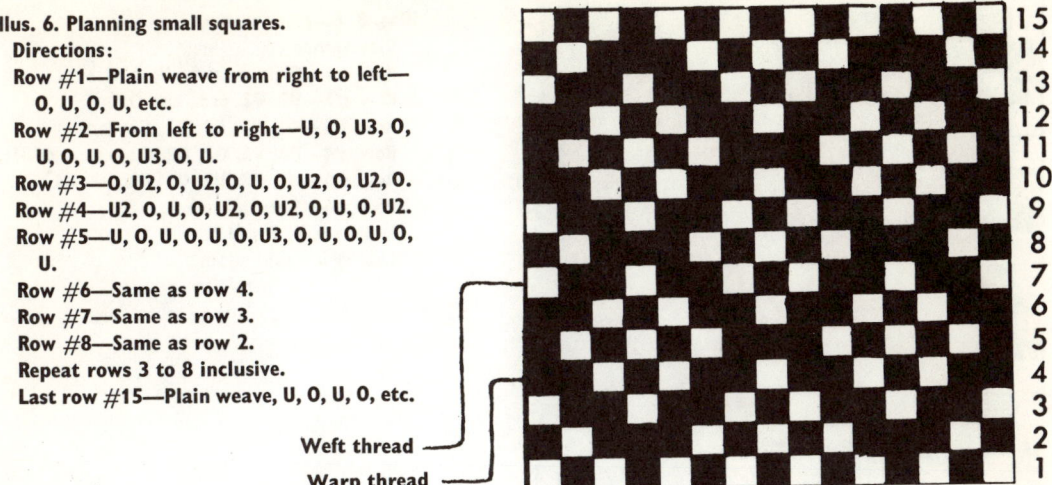

show, and vice versa. Where the warp will show, color the graph square solid. Where the weft thread will show, leave the graph square blank.

Weaving graphs are usually read from right to left, and since weaving always starts at the upper right-hand corner of the loom, instruc-tions are planned to read back and forth—first to the right and then to left. Study the graphs and weaving directions in Illus. 5–10 carefully, and compare them with one another. This will give you practice in working with graphs and eventually planning your own. All of these

Illus. 7. Planning small squares.
Directions:
Row #1—Plain weave—U, O, U, O, from
right to left.
Row #2—From left to right—O, U, O, U3,
O, U, O, U3, O, U, O.
Row #3—U, O, U2, O, U2, O, U2, O, U2,
O, U.
Row #4—U3, O, U, O, U3, O, U, O, U3.
Row #5—Same as row 3.
Row #6—Same as row 2.
Repeat rows 3, 4, 3, 2, 3, 4, 3.
End with a row of plain weave.

Weft thread
Warp thread

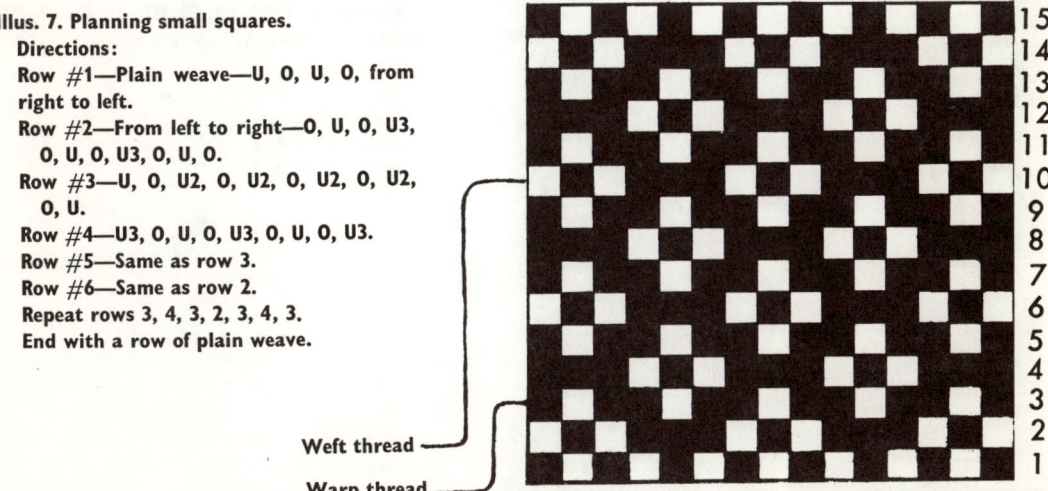

15
14
13
12
11
10
9
8
7
6
5
4
3
2
1

Illus. 8. Diagonal weave.
  Directions:
  Row #1—Plain weave—U, O, U, etc.
  Row #2—U2, O2, etc., end O1.
  Row #3—O1, U2, O2, U2, O2, etc.
  Row #4—O2, U2, O2, U2, O2, etc., end U1.
  Row #5—U1, O2, U2, O2, U2, O2, U2, O2.
  Row #6—Same as row 2.
  Repeat 3, 4, 5 and 2.
  Last row weave plain.

25	3
24	4
23	5
22	6
21	3
20	4
19	5
18	6
17	3
16	4
15	3
14	6
13	5
12	4
11	3
10	6
9	5
8	4
7	3
6	
5	
4	
3	
2	
1	

Illus. 9. Herringbone weave.
  Directions:
  Row #1—U, O, U, etc.
  Row #2—O2, U2, etc., end U1.
  Row #3—U1, O2, U2, O2, U2, O2, U2, O2.
  Row #4—O1, U1, O2, U2, O2, U2, O2, U2, O1.
  Row #5—O1, U2, O2, U2, O2, U2, O2, U2.
  Row #6—U1, O1, U2, O2, U2, O2, U2, O2, U1.
  Row #7—Same as row 3.
  Repeat 4, 5, 6.
  Repeat 3, 4, 5, 6.
  Repeat 3, 4, 3.
  Repeat 6, 5, 4, 3.
  Repeat 6, 5, 4, 3.

Illus. 10. Irish chain.

Directions:
Row #1—Plain weave, O, U, O, U, etc.
Row #2—U3, O, U3, O, U3, O, U3.
Row #3—O3, U, O3, U, O3, U, O3.
Row #4—U, O, U3, O, U3, O, U3, O, U.
Row #5—U3, O, U3, O, U3, O, U3.
Row #6—Same as row 4.
Row #7—Same as row 3.
Repeat 2, 3, 4, 5, 6, 3, 2.
Row #15—Plain weave, O, U, etc.

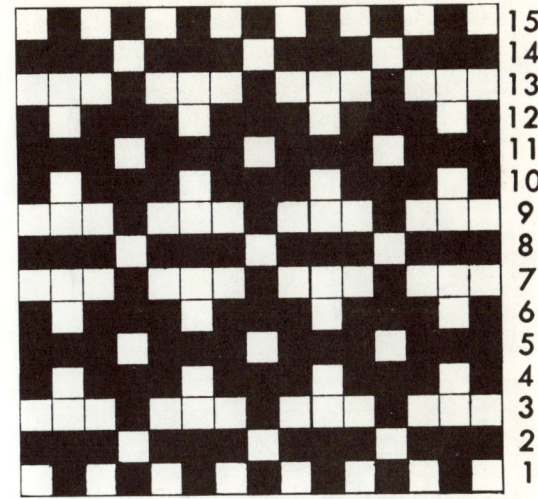

15
14
13
12
11
10
9
8
7
6
5
4
3
2
1

patterns are designed for weaving back and forth on the square weaver, and as in all weaving graphs, it is wise to make a few practice rows before attempting a project. Later on you may wish to weave these patterns on a four-harness loom (see page 16), but they will give you surprisingly good-looking results on your square weaver.

WHAT TO MAKE

The projects you can make on your square weaver are almost innumerable. Those that follow are only a few possibilities. Weaving is economical, too, for the amount of yarn required is less than half the amount commonly used in crocheting and knitting. You will also find your square weaver ideal for using up odds and ends of yarn, for you only need about four yards of yarn to make a 4″ square. Although you can use as many colors as you like in a square, the yarn should always be of the same weight and quality, or your square will be uneven.

An Attractive Scarf

Decide first how large you want the scarf to be. For children, 8″ (2 squares) in width and 32″ in length (8 squares) is a good size, while

Illus. 11. Scarf. Tie the strands with a slip knot, and make the knot as near the end of the scarf as possible. Trim the ends of the fringe so that all threads are of even length.

Illus. 12. Graph design for afghan.

making even a rather large blanket, since this consists of nothing more than a number of the squares you have already learned how to make sewn together.

Before you begin to weave, draw a graph containing as many squares as you plan to weave for the afghan. A good size is 16 4″ squares wide and 21 4″ squares long, but you may vary this according to your needs. A better size for a baby blanket is nine squares one way and eleven squares the other.

Plan on the graph (Illus. 12) the number of finished squares you will want in each color, and fill in each square with a crayon of the appropriate color, as shown in the illustration.

When your design is satisfactory to you, weave the squares, counting carefully to make sure you weave the right number of each color or pattern. If you do not have enough yarn for a solid color border, which requires 70 squares for the afghan and 38 for the baby blanket, buy three 4-ounce skeins of 4-ply wool for this purpose.

Sew all the finished squares together with matching colored yarn, and reinforce the outside edge by crocheting one row of single crochet stitches all round the edge.

Handbag or Knitting Bag

Make a paper pattern the size of the bag you want, making sure that it is at least two squares wider than the base of the handle you have chosen (Illus. 13). Divide the pattern into 4″ squares to determine the number of squares needed for the bag. Weave the squares into any design and sew them together with matching yarn.

Block the squares into shape, and add a lining of soft material. With matching yarn, fasten the lined squares to the holes which

an adult's scarf should be at least four squares longer. The width of an adult's scarf is optional.

Now plan your design. You might make an equal number of squares in tabby weave or two solid colors, which you would sew together alternately, fringing the ends of the finished scarf.

If you do not wish to use any of the designs you have learned from Illus. 5–10, this would be a good time to try an original design of your own. You could plan a design which would incorporate half solid color squares and half patterned ones, or weave all patterned squares.

An Afghan or Baby Blanket

An afghan is an excellent project for using scrap yarn, and after you have completed a scarf or two you should have little difficulty in most wooden or plastic handles have at $\frac{1}{4}''$ intervals for this purpose. A wide variety of handles is available at most department stores.

Berets for Children

An attractive beret (Illus. 14) is easy to make and a perfect gift for a child. It requires 13 4″ squares, and enough extra wool for a pompom on top.

Sew nine woven squares together to form a large square (three squares each way). Add a single square to the middle of each of the four sides of the large square (Illus. 15). Fold these back to form the underside of the beret. Next, fold the corner squares of the original large square diagonally across, turning them back so that their edges meet those of the undersquares (Illus. 16). Sew the matching loops together, starting at the beret's outer edge and working towards the middle, which will form the opening for the head. Sew each seam only half the length of the square, and fit the beret on to the head.

Determine now if the seam should be shorter or longer in order to make the opening fit the head, and make any necessary adjustments.

Illus. 14. Child's beret of small squares.

Illus. 13. Handbag of small squares.

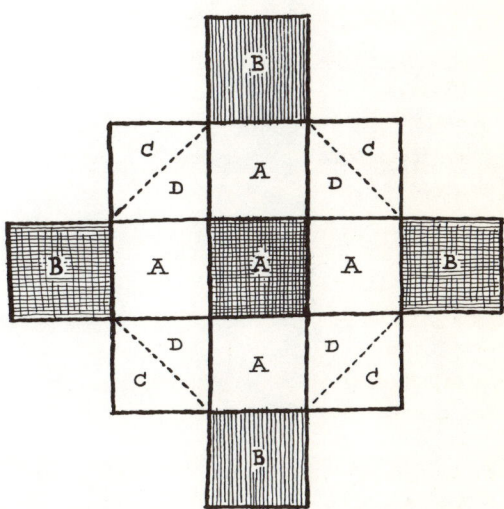

Illus. 15. Beret. Fold B over A, and C over D. Sew on wavy lines.

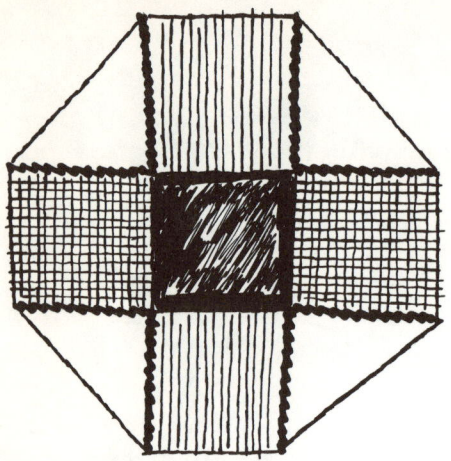

Illus. 16. Final shape of beret (from below).

Reinforce the beret's edges by overcasting them with yarn in a matching color.

The Pompom

To make the pompom, cut matching yarn into 4″ lengths. Tie a string of the same yarn round the middle of a group of 4″ threads, folding the ends together so the strands are all the same length. Wrap a piece of yarn several times round the top of the pompom, approximately $\frac{1}{4}$″ from the looped ends. Knot securely, and cut off any excess thread. Spread the strands to form a half ball, and trim the ends evenly. Using yarn and a large needle, attach the finished pompom to the top of the beret.

2. The Loom for You

In the small squares you have made so far, it has been very easy to interlace the weft with a small number of warp threads. However, making rugs, wall hangings, or simply a piece of material for a skirt requires such a large number of warp and weft threads that carefully going over and under each one would be an extremely tedious—if not impossible—process, even for the most dedicated weaver. Because

of this, our ancestors developed the loom, a device which simplified the weaving process.

As you know, a loom is a framework across which the warp threads are stretched and held taut while the weft, or *filling*, is being interlaced. To do away with the complicated process of going over and under every warp thread with the filling, looms have devices called *harnesses*, which lift alternate warp threads to form an

Illus. 17. Table loom with 4 harnesses.

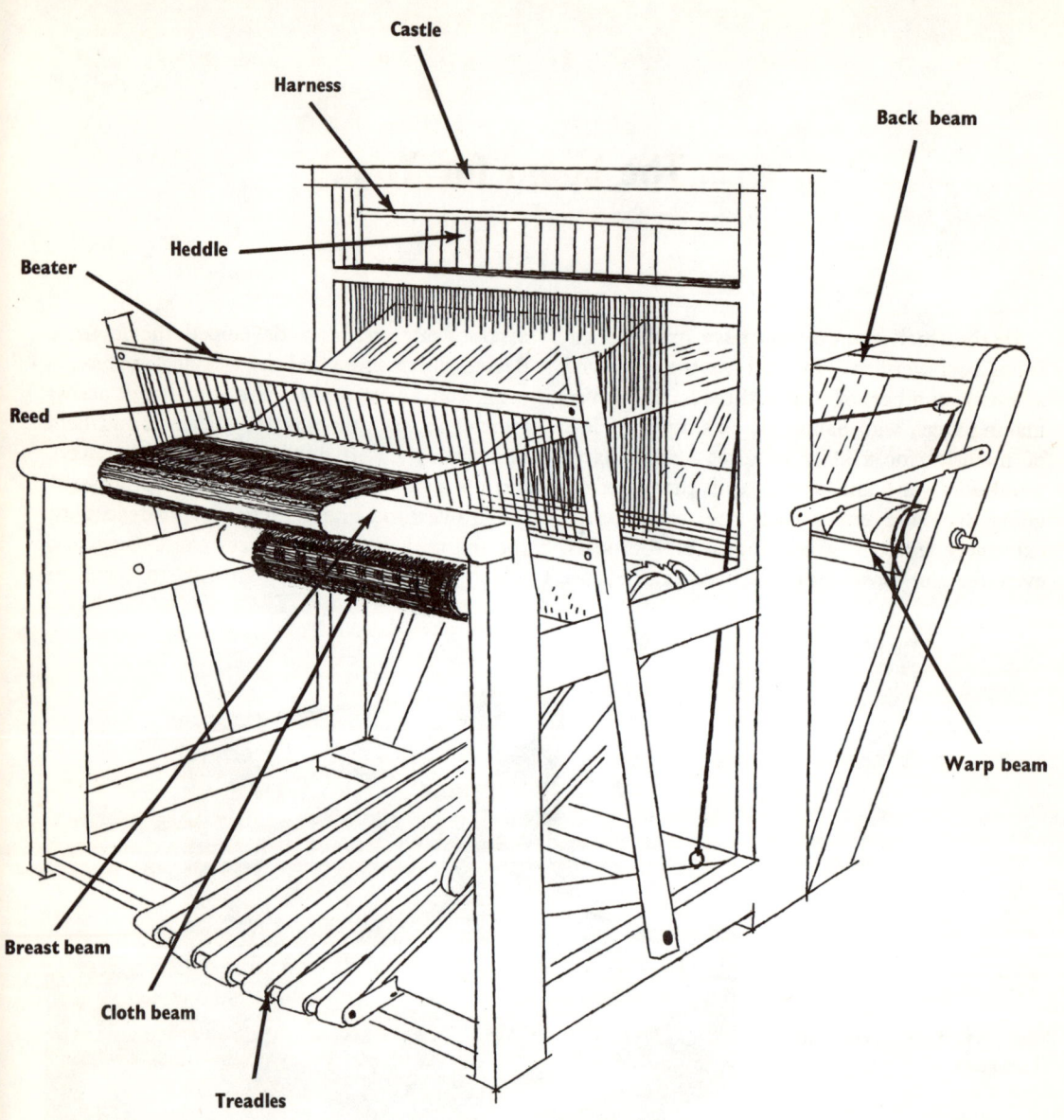

Castle

Harness

Back beam

Beater

Heddle

Reed

Warp beam

Breast beam

Cloth beam

Treadles

Illus. 18. Floor loom, 4 harnesses.

opening through which the weft can be passed in a single operation. This opening is known as a *shed*. At least two harnesses are necessary, for as you have learned, the second row of weaving must be opposite to the first. For the first row of weaving one harness lifts the *odd-numbered* threads to form a shed through which you pass the weft, wound round a *bobbin*, or *shuttle* (Illus. 22). In the next row of weaving, the other harness lifts all the *even-numbered* threads to form the second shed. When the shuttle is passed through it will go over all the threads it went under in the first row, and under all those it went over. The third row is formed just like the first row, the fourth like the second row, and so on. This alternation of sheds, then, while passing the weft through the openings, is weaving on a loom.

All looms, whether table or floor models, are the same in principle and will produce similar fabrics. That is, no matter what kind of loom is being used, a weaver always weaves a continuous weft thread back and forth across the long warp threads, through sheds provided by the various harnesses.

There are so many different styles of looms on the market today that it is not possible to give specific advice to the beginning weaver as to what type or size of loom to buy. It is not essential to begin weaving on a small loom and progress gradually to a larger one. Instead, choose the loom which falls within your price range, is best suited for the articles you want to make, and for which you have space available.

For example, if you want to weave articles no larger than table mats, scarfs, pillow covers, and handbags, a small, inexpensive table loom will be satisfactory. You can sew together strips of material woven on this type of loom to form larger articles, but the final result will not be as attractive as those woven in one piece on a larger loom. An ideal loom for the home weaver is a 32" or 36" table model with four harnesses (Illus. 17). On this loom you can weave narrow or wide materials, suiting, and large decorating fabrics.

Where to place a loom is always a problem, particularly for the city dweller who lives in a limited-size apartment. If you do have plenty of space, however, you will probably prefer to buy a floor loom. Although these are usually more expensive than table models, they have important advantages: both hands are left free for passing the shuttle through the various sheds, making the weaving process speedier and more rhythmic. This is because the *treadles*, which lift the harnesses, are pressed down with the feet in a floor loom. Table loom harnesses, on the other hand, are lifted by pressing down on levers by hand (Illus. 17). While weaving on a table loom can be perfectly satisfactory, obviously the floor loom is more comfortable to operate.

There are two kinds of floor looms: those in which when the treadles are pressed the harness is *raised* to form what is known as a *rising shed*, and those in which the harness is *lowered* when the treadle is pressed, forming a *sinking shed*. Looms with a rising shed are called *Jack-type*; those with a sinking shed are known as *counterbalanced looms*. Both looms are alike in every other way, and produce identical results. They are available in widths ranging from approximately 20" to 60".

If you have limited space but would still like to have a relatively large table or floor loom you should consider a folding loom (Illus. 19). A four-harness table model comes in 27" or 36" widths and weighs only 19 pounds. A Jack-type four-harness floor loom measures 20", 26", or 32", and is very compact when folded. These looms come with detailed instructions which explain how to fold them up, and are generally less expensive than most floor looms.

If you plan to use your loom to weave commercially, it should be quite strong and well made. A loom made of hardwood is the sturdiest of all, and will last a lifetime.

THE PRINCIPAL PARTS OF A LOOM AND HOW THEY FUNCTION

Before you begin to weave, you should become familiar with the parts of a loom and their functions, as frequent reference is made to them throughout the book. If you have never operated a loom, study Illus. 18 and 20 carefully before you begin to weave. Your patience at this stage will be rewarded with a firm background upon which to build your future weaving skills. Keep in mind that however complicated your loom might seem to you at first, it actually makes weaving simpler!

As you have learned, the principal function of a loom is to hold taut a series of long threads, or the *warp*, while loose threads, or the *weft*, are passed back and forth through them. Individual warp threads are called *ends*, and alternate ends are what the harnesses raise and lower to form the sheds through which the shuttle, carrying the weft threads, passes.

Since the warp is almost invariably longer than the loom itself, all looms provide a roller, the *warp beam*, at the back, round which the warp is wound until needed, and another roller at the front of the loom, the *cloth beam*, upon which the finished material is wound. Each roller is held in place with a lock, or *ratchet*. When more warp is needed, the ratchet is released so the warp beam can roll off the warp.

Illus. 19. Folding loom.

Harnesses are frames generally made of wood or metal. In order to hold the warp ends in the harnesses securely, it is strung with *heddles* (Illus. 21). Heddles are wire sticks with a hole, or *eye*, in the middle, through which the warp end is strung. Each heddle is fastened to a *heddle bar* at each end, which is in turn fastened to the harness frame. Floor looms usually have two, four or six harnesses (although some commercial looms have as many as 24), which are hung from a superstructure near the middle of the loom called a *castle*. As you know, the function of the harnesses is to form varying sheds through which the weft is passed. Harnesses are operated by foot treadles or hand levers, depending on the type of loom.

Another very important part of the loom is the *beater/reed*. Located in front of and parallel to the harnesses (Illus. 22), the *beater* is a wooden frame which holds the *reed*, a comblike device made of steel wires. The spaces between the wires of the reed are called *dents*. After the warp ends have been strung through the heddles, they are threaded between each dent, before being fastened to the *front*, or *breast*, beam. The reed keeps the warp ends parallel and properly spaced during weaving, so that they do not become gnarled or tangled with one another.

The other function of the *beater/reed* is literally to "beat" the weft threads into position after they have been passed through a shed. This is accomplished by pulling the beater towards the front of the loom after the shuttle has been passed through the shed (this is called a *shot*), and thereby pushing, or beating, the weft thread against the already woven material.

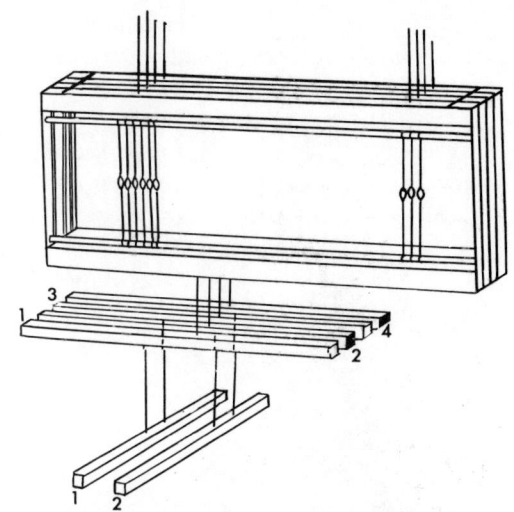

Illus. 20. Treadles, lams and shafts of a loom.

The beater should be pushed back to its original position before the shed is changed to weave the next row. Thus the procedure is to make a shed, "throw" a shot across the warp, "beat" the weft into place, and push back the beater. This is done for every row of weaving on a loom.

The only other major parts of the loom are the *apron* and *apron bars*, to which the unwoven warp is attached at each end. (You will learn

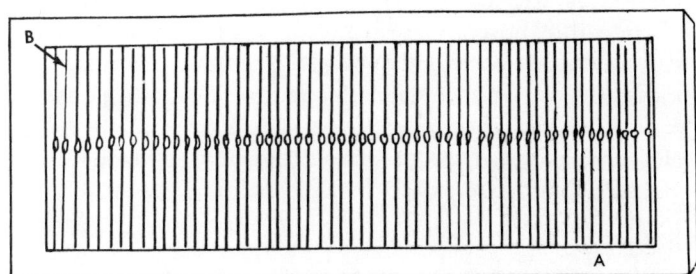

Illus. 21. Harness showing heddles.

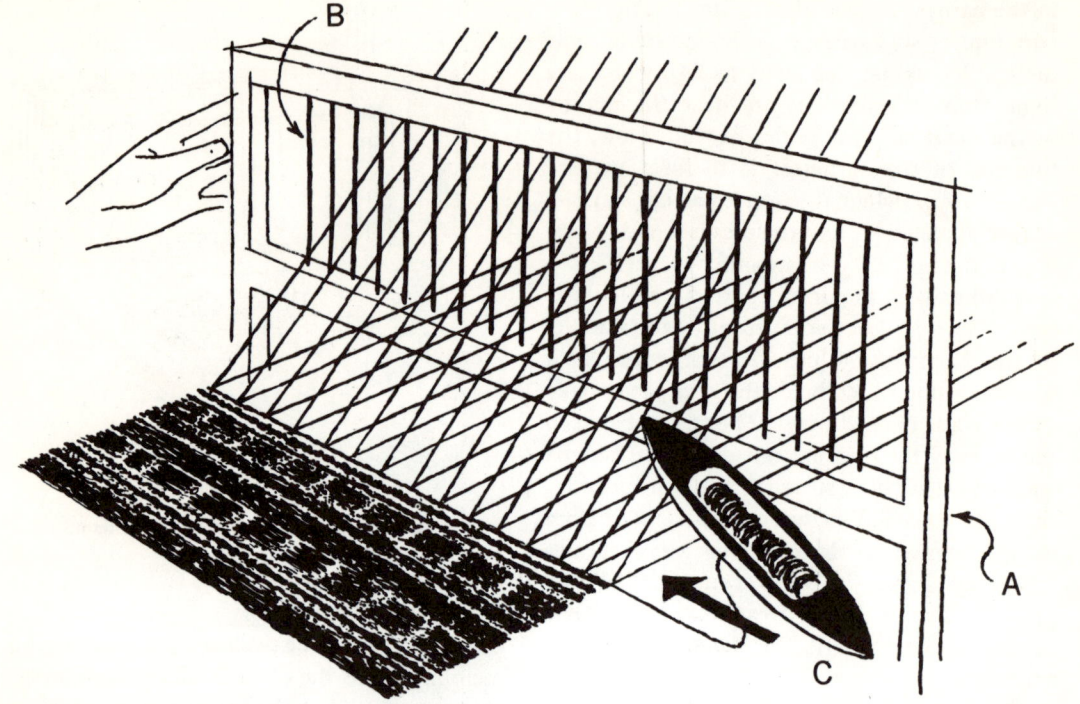

Illus. 22. The so-called beater/reed. A is the beater, B the reed and C is the shuttle entering the shed opening. A flip of the weaver's wrist will send the shuttle shooting all the way across.

how to attach the warp in Chapter Three.) The apron bars are slipped into the apron (Illus. 23), which fastens the bars to the warp and cloth beams at the back and front of the loom.

Looms usually come disassembled, and can easily be put together by following the accompanying instruction sheets and illustrations. No special tools are needed, and you should be able to assemble any loom without difficulty.

Certain basic equipment is also included with a loom, such as a *threading hook, lease sticks* (see page 25), and a *shuttle* (the different kinds of shuttles are described on page 35).

Now that you have learned how a loom functions, you are almost ready to weave. The one essential step before weaving, however, is preparing the warp and fastening it to the loom, which you will learn how to do in the next chapter.

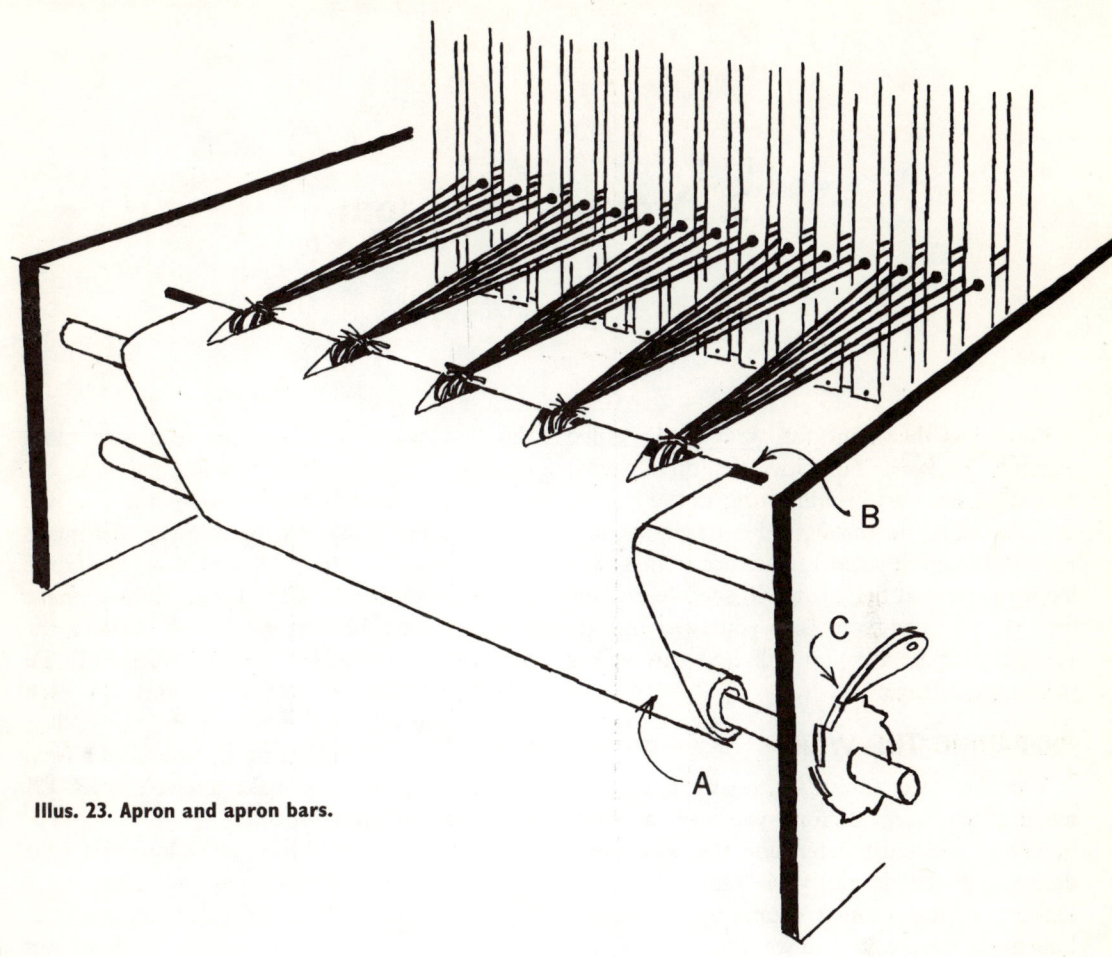

Illus. 23. Apron and apron bars.

3. Dressing the Loom

Preparing the loom for weaving is called *dressing the loom*. This involves three steps: preparing the warp, rolling it on to the beams, and threading it through the harnesses and reed. Although it requires patience to dress the loom properly at first, you will soon learn how important a good warp is to your weaving. As you gain experience you will find this task a pleasant challenge.

PREPARING THE WARP

The first step towards dressing a loom is making the warp. Before you can do this, however, you must determine the width and density of the fabric you want to weave. Density in this context means approximately how many warp ends you want to have to each inch of width of your fabric. A good number for most fabrics is 15 warp ends to the inch, but for a loosely woven fabric you might want only 5 or 10, and for a linen fabric you could want as many as 30. The number of warp ends to the inch (this is known as the *sett*) is also affected by the kind of material with which you will be weaving. Obviously a thick yarn 15 ends to the inch will not produce the same fabric as a very thin yarn 15 ends to the inch. For your first projects, a 2-ply wool yarn is probably

the best material to use, as wool has more elasticity than any other weaving material.

To find out how many warp ends you will need, multiply the sett, or number of threads to the inch, by the total width of the fabric you want to weave. Thus if you want to make a man's scarf 12″ wide, with 15 ends to the inch, you will need 180 (12×15) warp ends. To this you must add an extra end for each *selvage* (the edge of the woven fabric), which is woven double for strength. So you need a total of 182 warp ends to make a man's scarf 12″ wide, 15 ends to the inch.

The next step is to decide how long you want the scarf to be. To this figure you must add a *loom allowance* of 24″ or 36″, depending on the size of your loom. The purpose of this extra length is to provide for the following:

- The length of warp between the warp beam and the shed opening which cannot be woven into the fabric at the finish.
- The amount of warp used to knot ends to the warp and cloth beams.
- An allowance for hems or fringes.
- Take-up, which is the shrinkage that occurs when the tension is released as the cloth is cut from the loom. This varies according to the elasticity of the material,

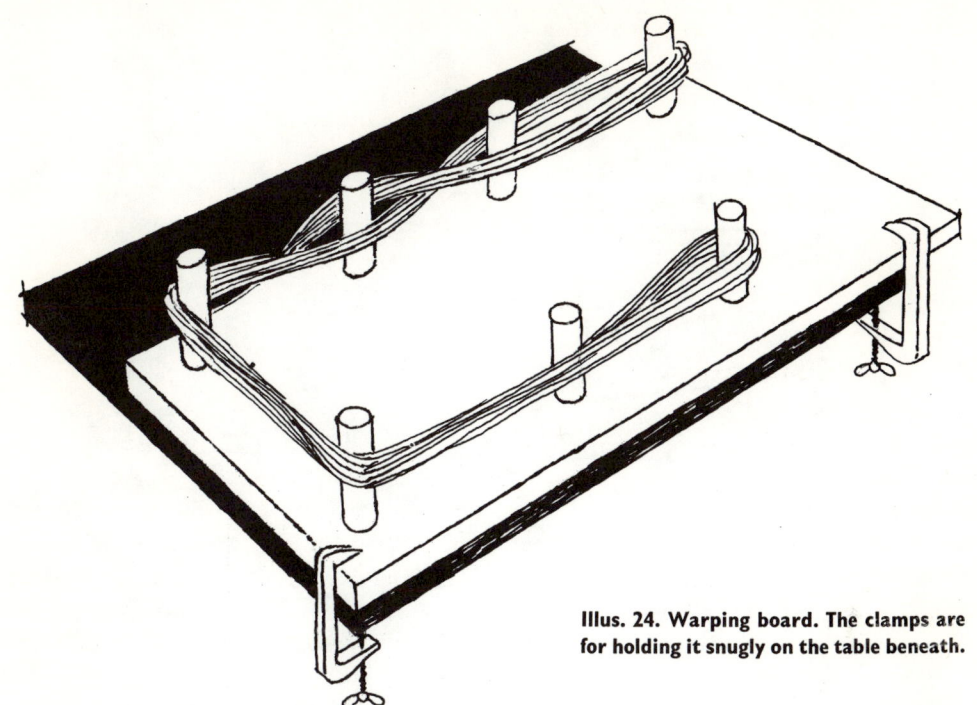

Illus. 24. Warping board. The clamps are for holding it snugly on the table beneath.

but you should allow at least 4″ to 5″ per yard for wool, which will "shrink" the most.

Let us say that you want your finished scarf to be 60″ long. Add the 36″ loom allowance to this, which means you will need a warp 96″ long and 182 warp ends wide. In order to prepare these, you will need to wind the lengths of warp on a *warping frame*.

The Warping Frame

The traditional method of preparing warp ends for a loom is to use a *warping frame* (Illus. 24). The purpose of the warping frame is two-fold. It makes it easy to measure your 182 96″ warp ends, and ensures that each warp end

will have the same tension as the next. If you cut 182 pieces of yarn 96″ long and fastened each one to your loom, you would not only be very tired, but you would have a warp with extremely uneven tension. Winding the warp in one piece on a warping board at 96″ intervals accomplishes both needs in very little time.

There are several kinds of warping frames available today, and all of them perform the same function. As a matter of fact, you can even wind warp round two chairs, although this is a much slower process. A good frame for the beginner is one which has holes bored at intervals through which warping pegs can be fitted. This will allow you to make an accurate measurement of the warp. You can make your

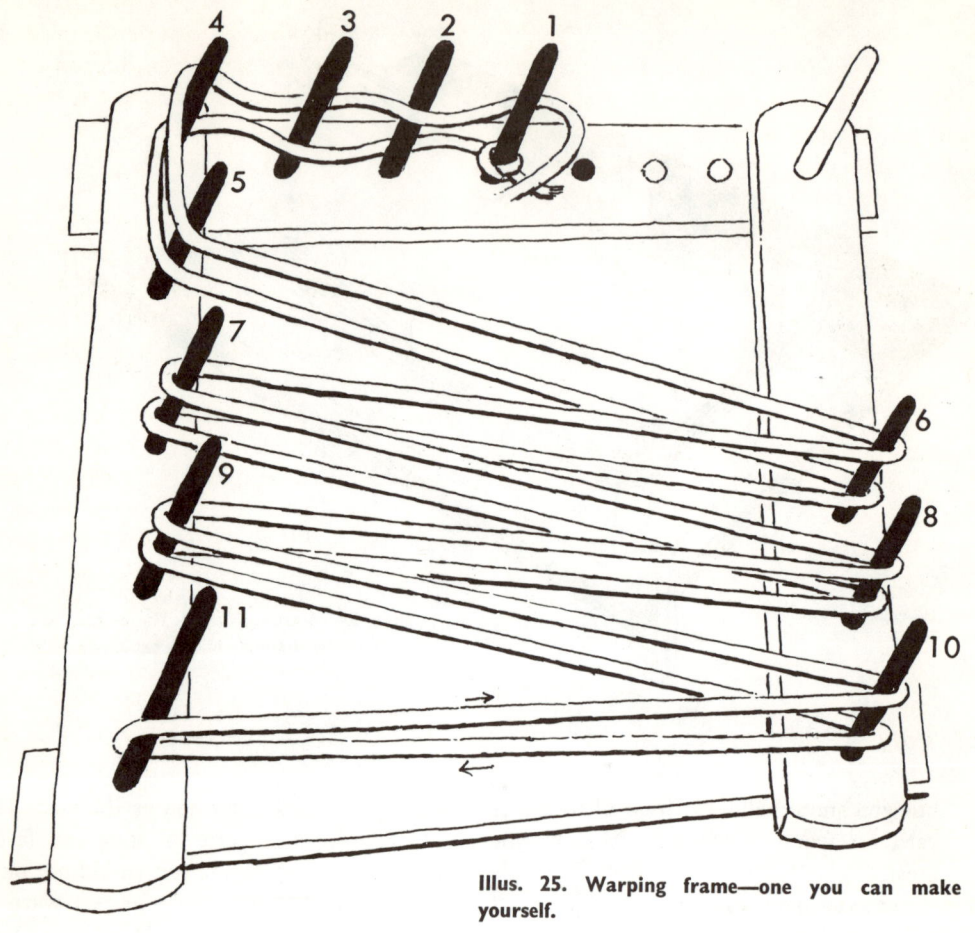

Illus. 25. Warping frame—one you can make yourself.

own warping frame (Illus. 25) in any size you want—in 5, 8, 10 or even 12 yard lengths—but 8 or 10 yards is sufficient.

You can see in Illus. 24 and 25 that on both warping boards the first three pegs are placed so that the warp threads will cross to make definite openings. This *cross*, or *lease*, is crucial, for without it the warp would be useless. The cross provides openings for the *lease sticks* (Illus. 28), which you will insert later on to keep the wound threads separate—some up and some down—while you thread the loom. Without the cross it would be impossible to keep the warp threads from tangling.

Winding the Warp

Before you begin to wind the warp, tie a bright colored string the length of the desired warp to the first warping peg and carry the string round the pegs to act as a guide for winding the warp. The placement of pegs in a warping frame varies according to different manufacturers' and weaving books, but the principle is the same.

Route of Warp Round Pegs

Tie the warp thread securely to peg No. 1 (Illus. 25). Carry it *over* peg 2, *under* 3, *over* 4, *then* down and *under* 5. Next take it across the frame to 6, and back over to 7, and so on until peg 11 is reached. Go *round* this peg and retrace the guide string back to and over peg 4. Now look again at Illus. 25 and note that the warp should go *over* 3 as well, then under 2, and round 1 at this point, ready to begin its second round.

If your frame is a small one, you will have to add extra pegs to make sure you have your 96″ length.

Handling the Warp Threads

Every warp thread must be of equal tension and length, so it is very important that the warping be done by one person only. Usually the warp thread is fed from the left to the right hand, which guides it round the pegs. *Try to maintain an even tension as you wind.*

Tying the Warp

In Illus. 26 you can see a detail of how the warp threads between pegs 2 and 3 make openings for the two lease sticks. To make doubly sure that you will not lose the lease cross in the warp, tie two pieces of different-colored string through the cross, one on each side. Be sure *not* to make a square knot—use a regular bow knot, so that it can be untied easily and not have to be cut. A security thread should also be tied between the two lease openings at the point where the threads cross.

It is also a good idea to count the warp ends as you go along so you will have a record for the final counting. One way to do this is to tie a string round each group of 20 or 25 threads as they are wound. This should be done at either the first or last peg in the warping frame.

Chaining the Warp

In order to transfer the warp to the loom without tangling, it will be necessary for you to

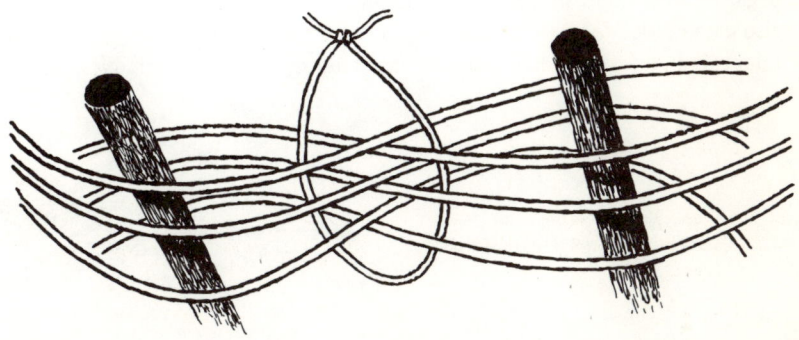

Illus. 26. Detail of opening between pegs for lease sticks.

Illus. 27. Chaining the warp.

chain it (Illus. 27). The first step is to tie strings round the loops at the first and last pegs, to hold them in place for chaining. It is also a good idea for a beginner to tie the warp at intervals between the pegs to prevent tangling.

To chain the warp, you will use your hand like a crochet hook. With the left hand, firmly grasp the warp in front of the last peg. Using your right hand, remove the peg from the warping board. Now make a loop over the back of

Illus. 28. Inserting the lease sticks at Peg No. 1 to hold the cross.

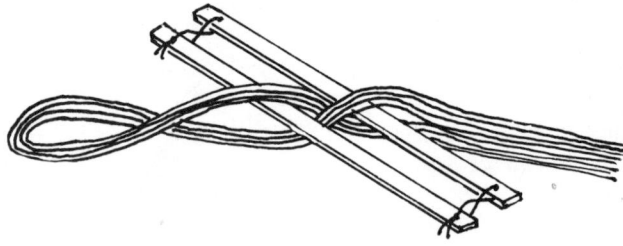

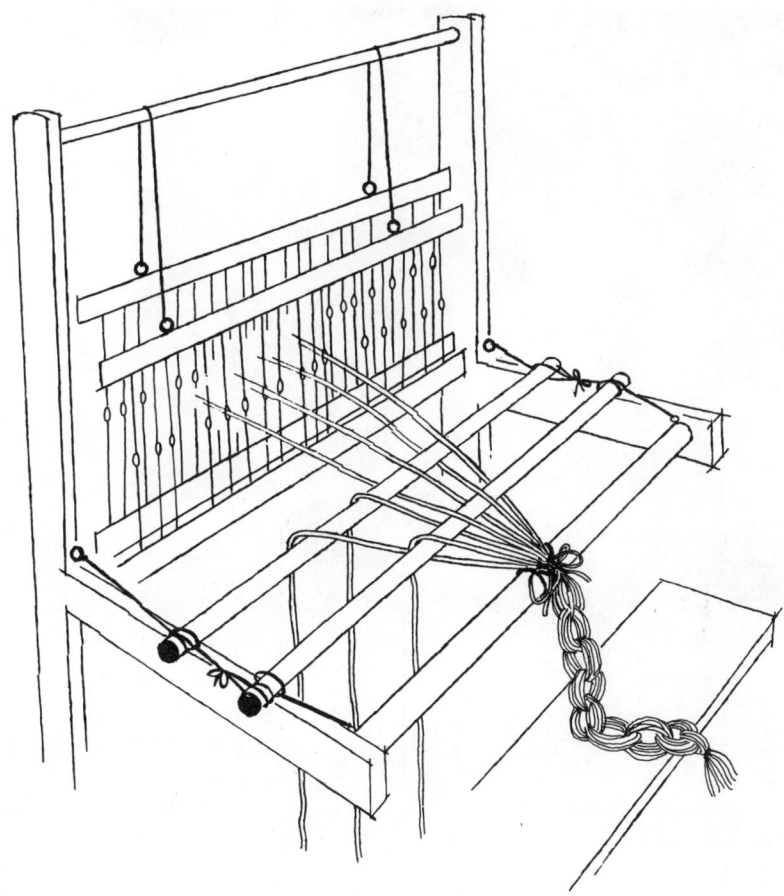

Illus. 29. The chained warp.

your hand, and pull the warp through so that it forms another loop. Continue looping until you have reached peg No. 1, but do not pull the last loop through or you will "lock" the chain and be unable to attach it to the loom. Peg No. 1 is where the warp has been tied to indicate where the lease sticks will go to hold the cross. After you have inserted the lease sticks (Illus. 28), the chained warp is ready to be transferred to the loom for threading.

THREADING THE LOOM

The loom can be threaded from either the front or the back, although most experienced weavers prefer the back-to-front method. However, it is best that a beginner first learn to thread from the front in order to understand completely the functions of certain parts of the loom. After you have thoroughly learned the process, you may thread from the back, because

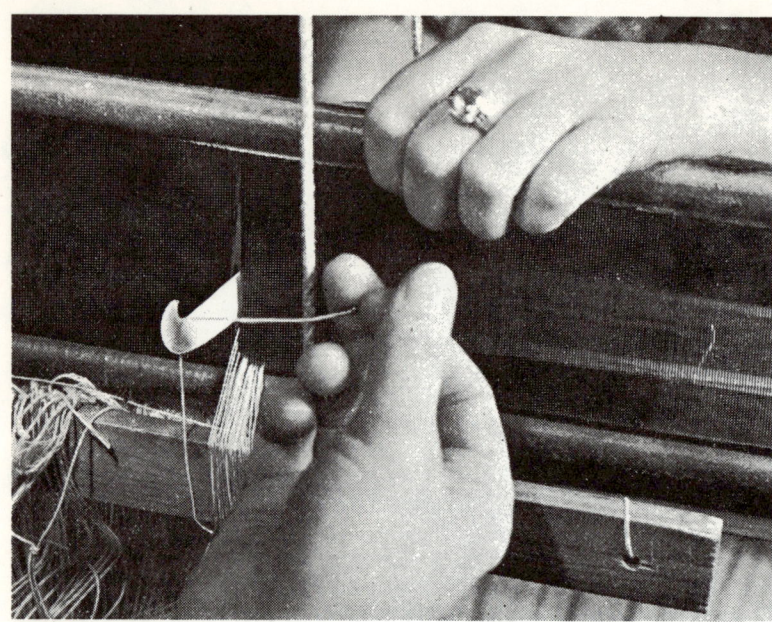

Illus. 30. Threading the warp through the reed.

you will then know the why and what of every operation.

Both methods have some special advantages. If one person has to thread the loom alone, threading from the front can be accomplished more easily. Also, a short warp, such as is used on table looms, is usually threaded from front to back.

Threading from the back, on the other hand, requires that two persons work together, especially on a 4-harness loom. However, it is definitely recommended that long warps with many threads be threaded from back to front.

What is most important is the result either method brings at the end. In order to attain quality in a piece of woven cloth, the warp must be at *even tension* in all places and at all times. The warp threads must be evenly spaced and parallel to one another, as well.

Warping from the Front of the Loom

The first step is to insert the two lease sticks in each side of the cross in the warp (Illus. 28). Tie the ends of the sticks together about 1" apart as shown in Illus. 28, and tie the lease sticks to each side of the loom between the breast beam and the beater/reed. The cross is now secure and the strings you tied round the cross on the warping frame can be removed.

Unchain enough warp so that the ends will reach several inches beyond the harnesses towards the back of the loom. Then secure the remainder of the chain to the breast beam. Cut the loops at the end of the cross facing the back of the loom, and spread the threads out evenly. You are now ready to thread the ends through the dents in the reed, a procedure called *sleying*.

Centering the Warp

The warp should always be threaded as near the middle of the reed as possible. To center the warp, you must count the total number of threads in your warp (182 for the scarf), and then count the number of dents per inch in your reed. The number of dents per inch, as well as the length of the reed, is stamped on the wide metal bar at one end of the reed. Available in a number of sizes, reeds can have from 12 to 15, 20 or more dents to the inch. The standard size is 15 dents to the inch, and if you have only one reed, it should be of this size. For fine linen weaving you can still use your 15-dent reed by running two, or even three, threads through every dent (*double sleying*), while for an open pattern or a loosely woven cloth, you can thread every other dent (*half-sleying*), in order to make your reed more versatile. For most work, one end is threaded through each dent, and you will want to do this for your scarf.

Let us assume that your reed has 15 dents to the inch and that the reed itself is 36″ wide. To find out how many empty dents to leave on either side of the warp in order to have it centered, multiply 15 (dents) by 36 (inches wide), and you will find you have 540 dents. Since you have only 182 warp ends, subtract this figure from 540, or the total dents, and divide the result by two, to determine how many empty dents must be left on each side. Your final answer should be 179 (358 divided by two). Count in 179 dents from the right (the loom is always threaded from right to left), and mark the dent lightly with a colored pencil. This is where you will begin threading the warp.

Sleying

Threading the warp through the dents in the reed is called sleying or *drawing-in*. Begin by drawing the first two warp ends as they come from the right side of the lease sticks through the first dent in the reed. This double sleying will form the selvage. Continue threading a *single* end through each dent in succession until you come to the last two threads which should be drawn in together to form the left-hand selvage.

It is important to take threads *in succession* from the lease sticks: first a thread from over the first stick, and the one from over the second stick, and so on. This will keep the threads in order for the next operation, which is to carry the ends through the heddles on the harnesses.

Illus. 30 shows how to use the hook which came with your loom to draw the warp ends

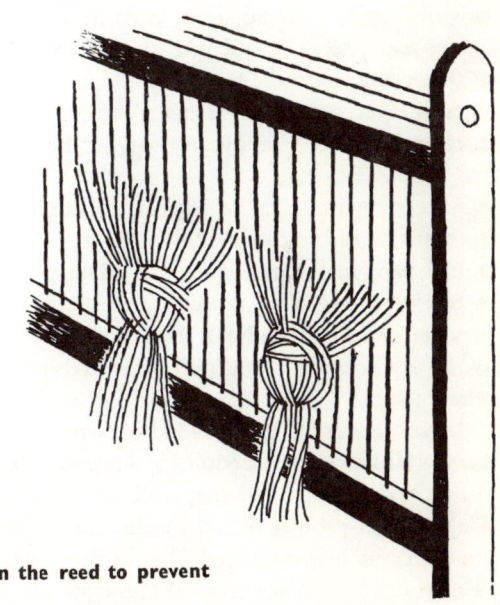

Illus. 31. Tying the warp ends in the reed to prevent slipping out during sleying.

through the dents. As you go along, tie small groups of threads together in loose knots at the back of the reed. Illus. 31 pictures how this prevents the ends from slipping out during the sleying process.

Threading the Harnesses on a 2-Harness Loom

Push the reed back close to the breast beam and tie it to the sides of the loom. This will provide more space to reach the heddles. As this is to be a threading which will produce a plain or tabby weave, you will not need a threading draft as you would for pattern weaving on a 4-harness loom. (We will explain drafts later on.) For a tabby weave you must thread alternate ends in alternate harnesses.

Working from right to left, select the first two threads for the selvage, and thread them through the first heddle on the right-hand side of the harness nearest the front of the loom (Illus. 32). Except for the selvage on the other end, from now on you will thread single ends in alternate harnesses. The next end, therefore, should go in the second harness, in the heddle farthest to the right (refer to Illus. 32 again), the next end next to the second heddle in the front harness, and so on.

Threading the heddles is done by inserting the warp thread in the heddle eye as you would thread yarn in a darning needle. Make a loop in the warp end, and, holding it in place with your left hand, pass a hook through the heddle eye to catch the loop and pull it through to the other side.

As you go along, it is a good idea to tie the warp ends behind the heddles in groups as you did on the reed, so that they will not pull out. Tie them in groups of 15, or the number of dents per inch in the reed. This will make it easy to check and see that all the ends are in

order. Checking dents and heddles carefully as you go along is absolutely essential to prevent trouble later on.

Tying on the Ends

The warp is now ready to be tied on to the back roller. Untie a group of threads behind the harnesses and measure to see if they are long enough to reach the back beam with enough extra length to tie round the apron rod. If not, untie each group and pull enough thread forward from the warp chain at the front of the loom. Then bring the roller apron up over the back beam and tie the apron rod in place.

Tie the first group of warp ends round the apron rod (Illus. 33). Be sure they are quite even and *all have the same tension*. Undo the group of ends to the extreme right and tie them to the other end of the apron rod. Continue with the middle groups until all the warp ends are tied.

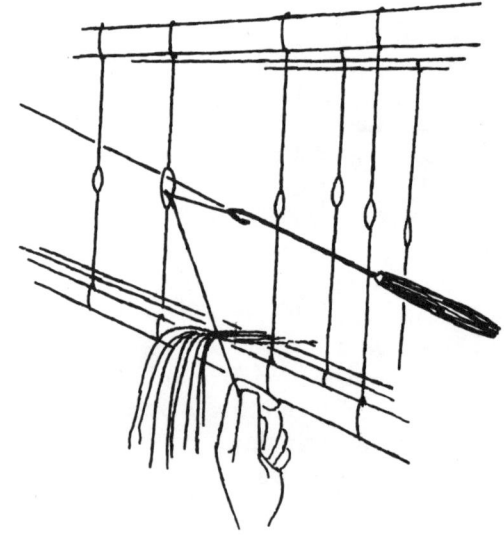

Illus. 32. Sleying harness.

30

Illus. 33. Tying warp on to front apron rod.

To tie the ends, bring each group in turn down over the apron rod, separate them into two equal parts, and pass the ends back up on either side of the group. Tie the ends together with a square knot as shown (Illus. 34), making sure first that all the ends are even.

It is a good idea to turn the warp roller a few notches at this point, giving the warp a final pull to see if all the warp threads are in order. If any of the groups or individual ends seem slacker than others, undo the knot and make the adjustment.

BEAMING THE WARP

Beaming is the action of pulling and winding the warp ends on to the back of the loom in preparation for weaving. If you can find a helper, well and good, but it is possible to perform this operation by yourself by following these step-by-step directions.

1. Have at hand sheets of heavy glazed paper and a number of tie-in sticks to be inserted, between the warp layers as it is being fed on to the back roller. The sticks should be about $\frac{3}{4}''$

Illus. 34. The square knot.

wide and the same length as the width of the warp beam. The purpose of both the paper and tie-in sticks is to hold the threads at even tension and to prevent soft yarns from pressing down on one another.

2. If everything is in order, you can begin to wind your warp on to the back roller. This will entail combing the warp with your fingers, or shaking out any tangles as you wind. Remember that all the ends must be at the same tension or you will have trouble later on. The tension can be adjusted by pulling hard on the warp threads at the other end of the loom, just in front of the lease sticks.

3. Untie the lease sticks from the sides of the loom. Leave them in place in the warp, and tie the ends of the sticks together, so they will not slip out. Unchain as much of the warp as can be used at one time (about 18"), and pull it out with both hands until the tension is even and all threads are in line. Shaking the warp will help to organize it, and pulling the lease sticks down towards you will also do the trick.

4. Now go to the back of the loom and turn about one-half yard of the warp on to the roller. Put in the padding paper and one of the tie-in sticks to keep the warp at the proper width. If you fold a hem about 1" wide every second or third sheet, it will be sufficient to hold the ends within the designated width.

5. Return to the front of the loom, grasp the warp chain, and pull on it very firmly, to tighten the warp. The lease sticks, the reed and the heddles have already done part of this, but not enough. Then pull the lease sticks towards the back of the loom another 18", straighten the warp if necessary, and again roll 18" on to the back roller. Continue unchaining as required and winding until the shortest warp ends hang just over the breast beam.

6. Tie the warp ends to the cloth beam rod as it is carried through the hem in the apron. If there are ragged ends, trim them off evenly. If the warp has been kept under perfect tension throughout, all ends will be approximately the same length.

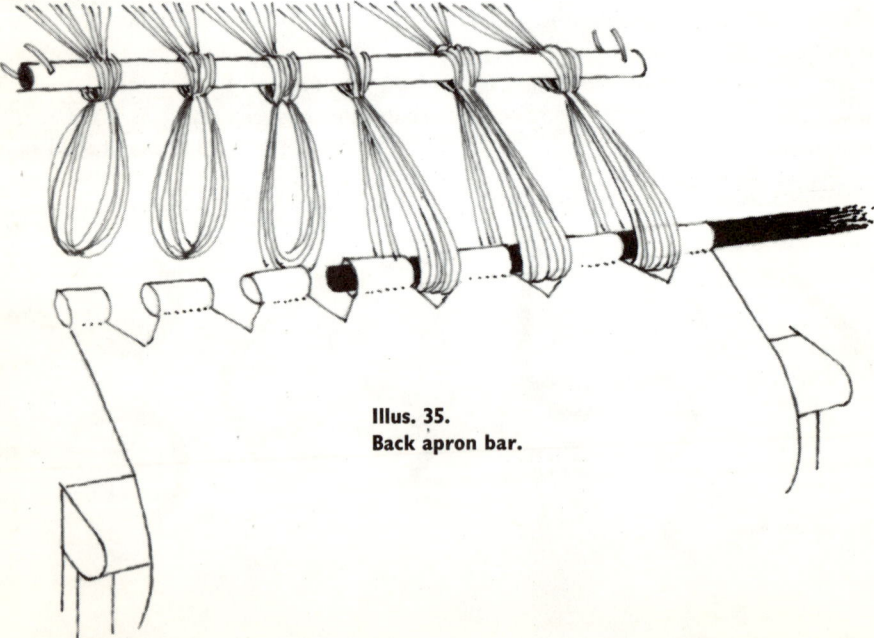

Illus. 35.
Back apron bar.

Table loom.

Woven knitting bags and
tablecloth.

Plain weave with vertical stripes made on a 2-harness loom.

Bands woven on 2-harness loom.

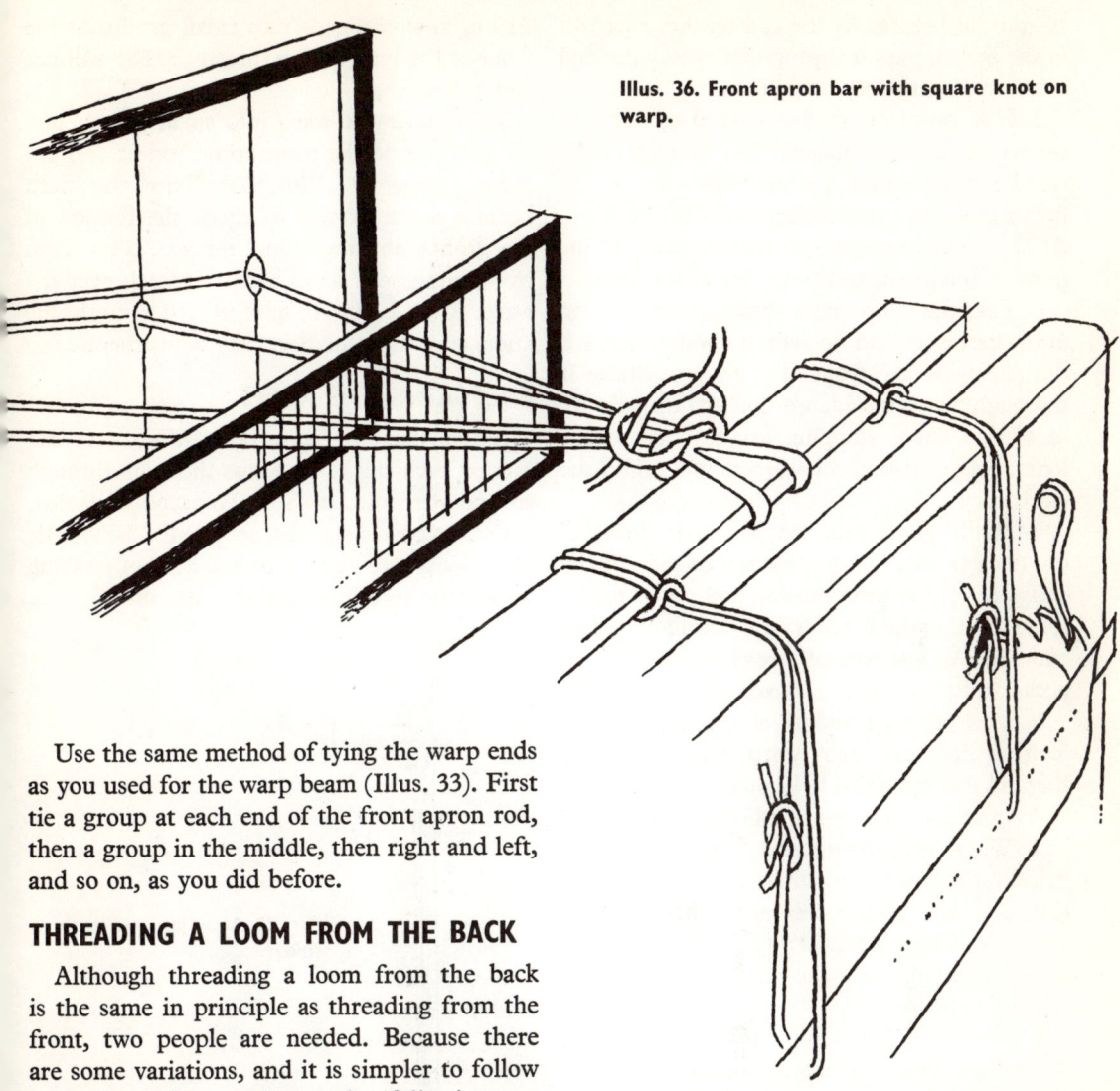

Use the same method of tying the warp ends as you used for the warp beam (Illus. 33). First tie a group at each end of the front apron rod, then a group in the middle, then right and left, and so on, as you did before.

THREADING A LOOM FROM THE BACK

Although threading a loom from the back is the same in principle as threading from the front, two people are needed. Because there are some variations, and it is simpler to follow uninterrupted procedures, the following are step-by-step directions for the back-to-front method, but with less detail.

1. Insert the two lease sticks through the cross in the warp chain, and tie them together at both sides to keep them from falling out of the chain.

2. Attach the loops at the end of the chain (in front of the cross) to the rod in the back apron (Illus. 35). This eliminates tying individual groups of warp ends with square knots,

as you did before. As the rod reaches each slit in the apron, pass it through an evenly divided number of warp loops as shown.

3. Now push the heddles toward each end of the harnesses, thus making an opening in the middle of the frame. Tie the beater/reed to the breast beam to make a clear path for the warp. At this point, one person should stand at the front of the loom, and the other at the back.

4. Pass the warp chain through the opening in the harnesses and unchain it enough to reach the person at the front of the loom. Shake it thoroughly and make sure that the threads are in order. Then, standing at the back of the loom, begin to wind the warp slowly round the back roller.

5. While you wind, the person in front of the loom must pull on the warp so that all the ends are held at even tension and go on to the roller in the right order and parallel to one another. Add sheets of heavy paper and an occasional tie-in stick as described on page 31.

6. The person standing at the front of the loom, if there are many warp ends, can divide them in two parts and hold them in both hands as in grasping the reins of a horse.

7. When the warp ends reach the space behind the harnesses, they are ready to be threaded through the eyes of the heddles. Tie the ends of both lease sticks firmly to the sides of the loom to hold the warp ends in order during the threading.

8. Now thread the ends through the eyes in the heddles exactly as you did on page 30. Continue until all the ends are alternately placed in alternate harnesses, remembering to double the ends at the selvage.

9. Each warp end must now be threaded through the dents in the reed, as in Illus. 30.

Again, knot the ends into small groups at the front of the reed as you thread so they will not slip out.

10. Divide the warp into small groups and tie each one to the front apron rod as you did before (page 31, Illus. 33). Turn the warp beam a notch or two to check the tension of the groups and individual threads. Test them by running your hand back and forth over the warp. If it is not in perfect order, untie the knots and make the necessary adjustments.

PREPARING THE WEFT

As you have learned, the weft is the thread carried back and forth across the loom through an opening called a shed. To accomplish this, various types of shuttles are used. The shuttle you choose will depend on the kind of weaving to be done and the size of the yarn used.

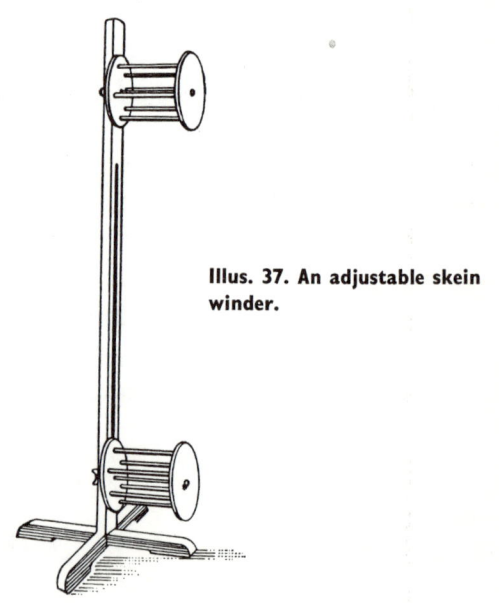

Illus. 37. An adjustable skein winder.

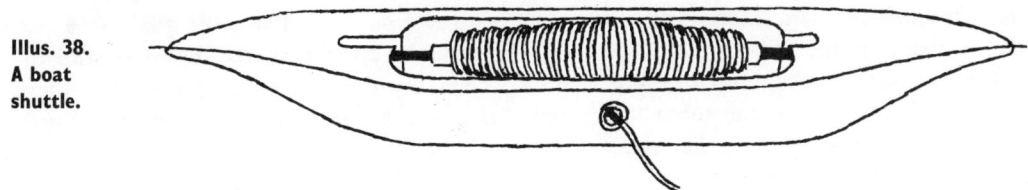

Illus. 38. A boat shuttle.

Threads used for the weft are usually taken directly from spools, skeins or balls. (If winding from a skein, you can use an adjustable skein winder like the one in Illus. 37 to make the necessary bobbins.)

The shuttle most commonly used in weaving average-size threads is called a *boat shuttle*, because of its shape (Illus. 38). This has a quill or bobbin which can be removed for winding on the weft. To remove the bobbin from the shuttle, grasp it in the middle and pull it up. Some shuttles have a rod which passes through the middle and is hinged at one end so that it can be removed at right angles.

A bobbin winder can be purchased at a reasonable price, and should be standard equipment for a weaver. The steellike rod which holds the bobbin is tapered so the thickest part

is near the wheel. By shoving the bobbin towards the heavier end, it is held tightly in place during the winding.

To wind the bobbin, place it on the shaft and push it towards the thickest end so that it will stay in place. Turn the handle of the wheel with your right hand and bring the thread *upwards* from the spool with your left hand. Hold it behind the bobbin at the left.

Turn this short end down over the bar and wind back and forth long enough to secure it in place. Now continue winding by turning the handle of the bobbin winder clockwise. The course of the thread should be guided gradually at first from left to right, then back and forth. First fill up the ends of the bobbin and then run the thread back and forth until all the threads lie in a straight line from end to end. The last

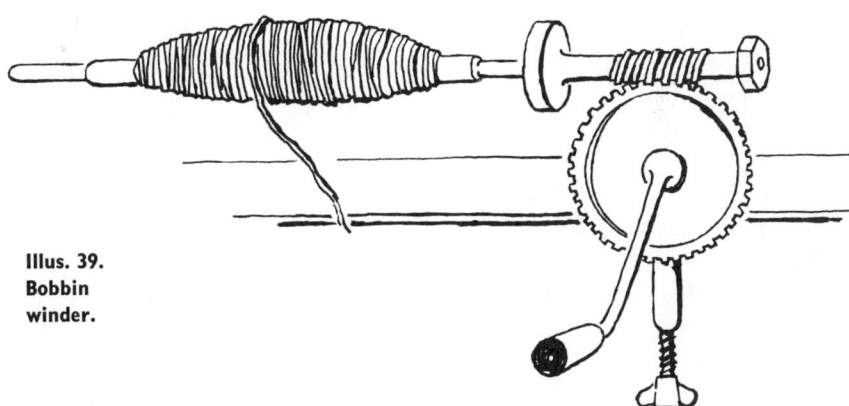

Illus. 39. Bobbin winder.

few turns will fill the middle, making it somewhat higher than the ends.

Remove the bobbin and slip it into the shuttle bar in such a way that the thread will come from underneath when the bar is snapped back into place. Pull the thread out through the hole on the side and the shuttle will be ready for weaving.

SECTIONAL METHOD OF WARPING

A sectional warping beam differs from an ordinary beam in that it is divided into 10 to 20 sections. The warp is kept in place in the various sections by means of wooden pegs. The threads are wound on to the beam directly from a spool rack and each section, in turn, is filled with the calculated amount of warp. This method is a definite time-saver for the weaver who uses a big loom with long warps.

The warp threads are wound on to the beam one section at a time. In order to keep the threads from twisting as they are being wound on, the weaver must use a guide of some kind. This is usually a flat piece of metal the width of the section in the beam and in it are punched

60 holes or more. Place the guide in a slot so it stands upright in the beam of the loom. The threads from the spools are threaded through the holes, beginning with the ones at the bottom of the rack. Care must be taken that all are held at equal tension.

In putting on a narrow warp that will not occupy the entire width of the loom, warp the middle section first and continue by warping first on one side and then the other until the required number is warped.

Some sectional beams have an indicator to help keep a record of warp length. If not, make a notation of the number of rotations made by the beam and multiply by one length of thread around it. As each section of the warp is completed, place some cellophane tape across the threads about 20″ from the beam. The length is needed to reach the heddles for threading and the tape will substitute for the lease sticks in keeping the ends in correct order.

Cut the warp and fasten it in place on the roller with a safety pin. This will prevent the ends from unwinding while other sections are being beamed.

4. Weaving on a Two-Harness Loom

Now that we have talked about the parts of a loom, how to dress it, and have made the necessary preparations for weaving, it is time to begin the actual weaving of the scarf.

Since the loom has just two harnesses, it will make only a plain or tabby weave, which you learned about in Chapter One. Any variations in the scarf must, therefore, come from color. You can have colored borders, stripes that run lengthwise or across the fabric, or heavy ridges known as *reps*, which are produced by threading a number of dents double. For this first project, let us try something simple by planning that the scarf will be green with narrow horizontal stripes of white at the ends.

THE FIRST STEP

Although the weaver usually begins by weaving in a few shots of candlewicking or rags in order to straighten out the warp threads, this is not really necessary with 2-ply yarn. Instead, plan to fringe the ends of your scarf. Thus, the first few rows will be unravelled later on anyway, to form the fringe.

To make the first row of weaving, press down the front harness★ and pass your shuttle wound with green yarn through the shed from

★ If you are working on a counterbalanced floor loom, see page 51 to learn how to attach the treadles to the harnesses.

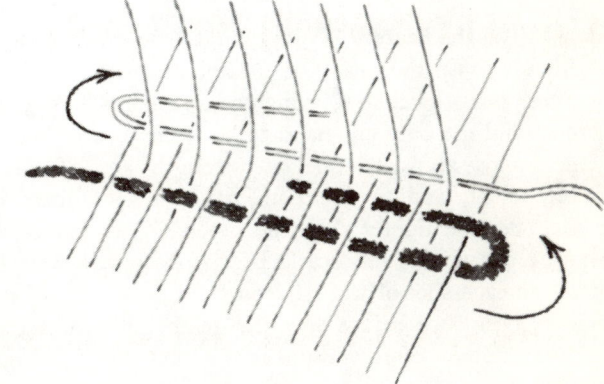

Illus. 40. Changing the weft to introduce a new color.

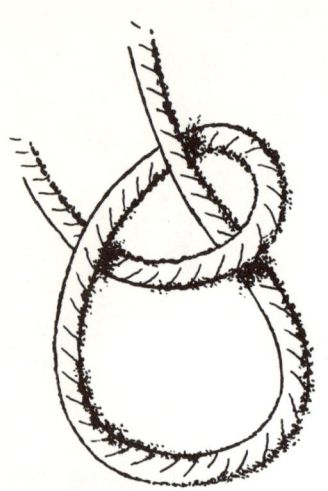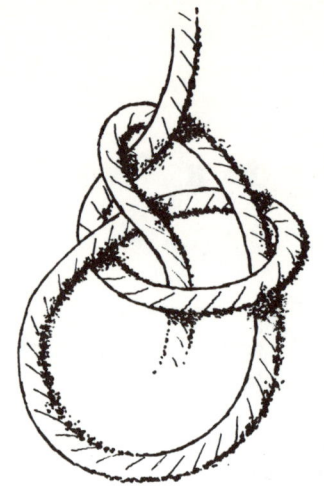

Illus. 41. The weaver's knot.

right to left, leaving about 2″ of wool outside the shed at the right, which you will weave in later. Draw the shuttle through so that it comes out on the other side leaving the weft thread in a slightly diagonal position, just as you did when using your square weaver. Now beat it in place with the beater/reed. Depress the back harness, pass the shuttle through the shed from the left to the right with the weft thread in a diagonal position, beat and go on.

How to Use the Beater

Always grasp the beater at the middle with your left hand. Even in weaving on large looms, you should use only one hand to beat, because your hands are not equal in strength and development, and to use both hands would make one side tighter than the other. If you want a loosely woven scarf, beat only once between each shot of weft. If you want a tight weave, beat once before you change the shed and once after, before you put in the next shot of weft.

Making a Good Selvage

Uneven selvages will form if the weft thread is either too loose or too tight. Loop the weft threads closely and evenly round the selvage threads of each row, forming an even row of loops. An uneven fabric is caused by pulling the weft thread more tightly in some places than in others. Remember, tension in weaving is all important. You must try to maintain an even quality at all times.

Changing the Weft to Introduce a New Color

After you have at least 6″ of woven fabric in green, it is time to begin adding the stripes. To do this, cut the green weft thread about 2″ from the right-hand selvage. Fold this end back over the warp when you form the next shed (Illus. 40). Bring across the new white weft thread from the *left*, and turn back the end as shown in Illus. 40. Change the shed and force the ends back with the beater.

In the future, you will plan all your weaving projects on draft paper first, but since you did not do so this time, you must measure each stripe and its distance from the beginning very carefully, so that you will be able to duplicate the pattern at the other end of the scarf. Check to make sure that you are weaving the same number of weft rows to the inch as you go along.

Adding color is where your imagination and creative instinct can come into play. It is one of the most rewarding aspects of weaving.

If a Warp Thread Breaks

A warp thread does break once in a while, but it is not difficult to remedy. If it breaks behind the harnesses, just wind a warp thread on to a spool heavy enough to give tension, and tie it to the broken thread with a weaver's knot (Illus. 41). Let the spool hang down over the beam. You will have to make a loose knot against the spool so you can lengthen the thread from time to time as the weaving proceeds. When you cut the finished scarf from the loom, poke the ends of the knot to the underside of the fabric.

Here is another version of repairing broken threads—one which eliminates tying knots. If a warp thread breaks, check its proper position and thread a new warp thread—which is wound around a spool—from the back through the heddle and the reed and fasten it to the web with a straight pin, winding the end of the thread around the pin like a butterfly. Weave

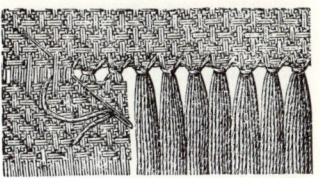

Illus. 42. A hemstitched fringe.

with this replacement thread until the other part of the broken thread can be tied to your web in the same way, then cut off the replacement thread. When the finished piece comes off the loom, the ends of these threads have to be sewn in.

Winding the Warp

When you have woven until your work gets too near the heddles to allow for a good shed, it is time to loosen the ratchets and wind the fabric on to the front roller. Before you do this, make sure you have carefully measured the amount of tabby at the beginning and the width of the stripes so they can be duplicated on the other end. Wind until about 1″ of weaving still extends beyond the breast beam, tighten the ratchets, and continue weaving.

The Fringe

A hemstitched fringe is best on a woollen scarf. It should be done while the scarf is still on the loom. Thread a needle with one of the plies from your green yarn, and run it along the left selvage to attach it (Illus. 42). Now pass the needle from right to left under two or three threads, draw it out, and pass it from below upwards and under one or two threads in the woven fabric. When you finish the hemstitching, weave another inch or two—however long you want your fringe to be. Run the needle containing the thread used for the hemstitching along the selvage to the end of your scarf, and fasten it with an overstitch.

Illus. 43. Small fringe knotted in two rows. Each knot is made with two groups of threads.

Illus. 44. Table mat painted on the warp with textile colors.

The next step is to cut the scarf from the loom. Since you did not hemstitch the fringe at the beginning (which you could have done), you must do it now. Hold the scarf wrong side up with the warp ends away from the body. Pass the needle with green weft thread between and round the same number of warp threads as you did at the other end, working from left to right. Bring the thread up to the surface and take a small stitch in the fabric.

Now ravel out the fringe as shown in Illus. 42. You should have a very attractive scarf.

ADDING NEW WARP TO OLD

If you are going to use the same warp threading in your next project, you can tie the new ends on to the old ones. Make a new warp chain and wind it loosely round the cloth beam. Insert the lease sticks and cut the loops in front, drawing the ends up just behind the heddles. Now tie the new to the old ends, being sure all are in proper alignment, with a weaver's knot (Illus. 41). After the knots have been pulled

through the heddles and reed, hold the new warp out at tension in front while it is being wound round the warp roller.

Textile Paints

Attractive table mats such as shown in Illus. 44 and other small articles can be decorated by painting the design on the warp under tension on the loom (before weaving). Either draw the design freehand or hold a picture under the warp and follow the outline, using the textile paints. Use of the extender sold with textile paints will help to hold the color.

After the warp is painted, make the colors very strong as they will be muted after weaving. Separate the warp threads by using a tabby treadle and prop the harnesses in this position until the paint is dry.

Weave with the same weight thread or finer (finer preferred) and use a rather light beat so as not to obscure the design too much.

After removal from the loom, pressing with a medium-hot iron tends to set the color too. These paints are washable with ordinary care.

5. Patterns to Weave on a Two-Harness Loom

It is very easy to add both color and texture to fabrics woven on a two-harness loom. Plain weaving can always be made interesting and attractive, not only by adding pattern threads for a design, but by making unusual arrangements of the warp. In a woven fabric, the line of direction can be vertical or horizontal.

There are many ways in which a design can be woven into a plain or tabby background. First of all, you have unlimited possibilities in the use of new and dramatic fibres such as Celanese, gold and silver metallic threads, and a milk fibre called Aralac, to name only a few. Plain weaves can have as their main interest contrast of texture: fine thread against coarse, shiny against dull, woolly against smooth, and so on.

Many designs possible on a two-harness loom are those in which the warp threads are arranged in patterns through the heddles and dents. Leaving some heddles and dents empty while threading others double is one example of this. Another popular design is one of vari-colored stripes or plaids. The possibilities are so numerous that they cannot all be described in one book, but the following basic variations will give you the knowledge and experience to weave any patterns contained in the books on your library shelves.

STRIPES

The simplest of all pattern effects is the use of broad and narrow stripes. Stripes had their beginning in ancient civilization. The Romans used vertical stripes in their draperies to dramatize heights of windows in their palaces. In India, weavers have long been famous for their finely contrasted colors and beautifully proportioned stripes.

Due to the large assortment of threads in dramatic colors and textures to choose from, bold stripes are used in many fabrics—even satin and velvet. Unless you have had some training in design, however, it is advisable to incorporate only a few colors in each stripe. The pattern can be accentuated by adding narrow lines of black and white, or metallic threads, which come in all colors.

The spacing and colors of stripes should be planned in advance, particularly if the stripes are to be woven vertically. Plot the exact number of warp threads necessary on graph paper, taking into account the number of dents in the reed. It is also wise to make a sketch in crayon,

Illus. 45. In a plaid pattern both the warp and the weft have the same number of different-colored threads.

to assure proper proportion and pleasing design. Horizontal stripes are simpler to weave, in that they do not require anything more than plotting on graph paper. Since vertical stripes require a multicolored warp, it is best to wait until you have woven a few articles and acquired some ease when working with the loom before attempting them.

Here are some of the ways to vary stripes in a fabric: alternate stripes of the same width and color; separate broad stripes with a narrow one; or separate broad stripes by several narrow ones in different colors. Whatever the pattern, the stripes must be placed in proper proportion to the design.

Ties

The standard length of a tie is 45 inches. These ties are sleyed rather coarsely in the reed and are woven in plain or tabby weave. If woven on a four-harness loom, two ties are usually set up several inches apart in width, for the purpose of balance. After weaving 15 inches, the weft is drawn in tighter so as to make the tie narrower, then the former width is resumed for another 15 inches.

PLAIDS

For plaids, both the warp and the weft are threaded in various colors. Both the warp and the weft must have the same number of different-colored threads (Illus. 45). The design of a plaid can be any arrangement of threads which pleases the weaver, as long as there are at least four colors involved in the design. Before you weave stripes, examine a piece of commercially woven material to study the arrangement of the different stripes and squares, and how the different-colored threads relate to one another. Colors in plaids change as often as every other thread sometimes.

When you wind the warp, tie on new colors at the first peg on your warping frame, with a square knot. If many colors are involved, the threads need not be broken at every color change. Just let them hang down from the peg, ready to be picked up again when needed. Place the cross in the warp at the opposite end from which the threads are started.

Illus. 46. Black-and-white check.

CHECKS

True checks (Illus. 46) are developed from a striped warp that has the same number of colored threads in the weft. As with all patterns based on variations of the warp, the squares must be planned on graph paper before the warp is wound. Block out the design carefully, after counting the total number of stripes that can be woven across the width of the material and counting the number of threads necessary for each check.

Illus. 47. Checked plaid design.

Treadles

1
1
2
2
1
1
2
2

Illus. 48. Basket weave on 2-harness loom.

Directions:

Tie up		Threading												
	1	2											
2		X				2	2			2	2		2
1	X							1	1			1	1	1

Checked designs can be varied in many ways. The colors can be evenly or unevenly divided, either two or more colors being alternated. The well known shepherd's plaid is made of $\frac{1}{4}''$ white and $\frac{1}{4}''$ black stripes in that sequence across the warp, separated in the weft the same way.

BASKET WEAVE

The basket weave is a form of tabby weave, except that two or three weft ends at a time are woven into double or triple warp ends (Illus. 48 and 49). Result is a loosely woven fabric ideal for lightweight wool blankets, crib robes, and the familiar drapery material known as monk's cloth (Illus. 50). This 2/2 combination is also used for weaving tightly twisted strands of worsted into a clothing fabric called hopsacking. Some basket weaves contain as many as six threads in each alternation.

When two or more weft threads are to be used, wind them on to the shuttle from two separate spools or balls. The warp ends must be threaded two to each heddle and dent.

When you are using more than one weft thread in a shot, be sure to arrange each thread

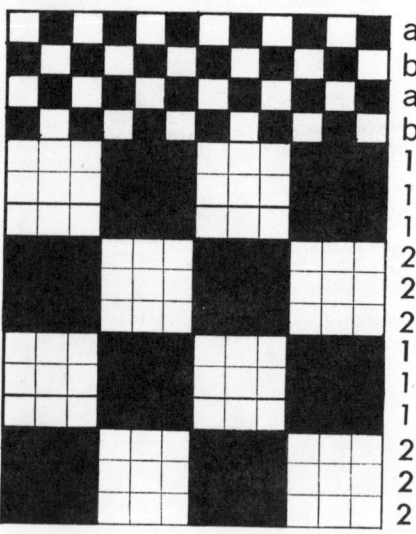

a
b
a
b
1
1
1
2
2
2
1
1
1
2
2
2

Illus. 49. Basket weave on 4-harness loom.

Directions:

Treadles			Tabby		Threading									
	1	2	a	b										
4		X		X		4	4			4	4			4
3		X	X				3				3			3
2	X		X					2	2			2	2	2
1	X			X				1				1		1

44

side by side in the shed before you use the beater. It is also necessary to pass the shuttle between the selvage threads on each side before throwing the shuttle through the shed. This will prevent the weft threads from pulling out as the weaving proceeds.

TEXTURE WEAVES

Plain weaving can always be made interesting by making special arrangements in the warp and weft. To leave spaces in the dents is one way of doing this; another is to thread a group of ends in a single dent and then skip a calculated number in between. No matter how the threads are sleyed in the reed, the same combination must be used in threading the heddles.

LENO

Leno is a general term used in weaving when a combination of tabby and rows of warp threads twisted together result in a gauzelike or lacelike fabric. The warp ends cross each other either in pairs or in other combinations, and the crosses are held in place by a weft thread.

Leno should be woven with slightly less tension on the warp than for plain weaving. Begin with the shuttle on the right-hand side. Open the shed, and make sure the outside thread on the right-hand side of your warp is *up*. Here is a basic leno pattern, 3 over 3 to begin with.

Illus. 50. Monk's cloth.

As in Illus. 51, hold an inch or more of the upper warp threads in your left hand, with the thumb on top and the second finger underneath, pulling slightly to the left, so that the lower threads are visible. With a pick-up stick (Illus. 52), pick up the 3 outer warp threads on the lower layer; then depress the 3 outer threads on the upper layer with the stick, passing the stick over these last 3.

Continue in the same way across the entire warp, picking up 3 from the lower layer and passing the stick over 3 from the upper layer. When you have completed the row, turn the pick-up stick on edge (Illus. 53), and pass the shuttle through the opening. Take out the stick and draw the weft thread tight enough so that all twists are flat.

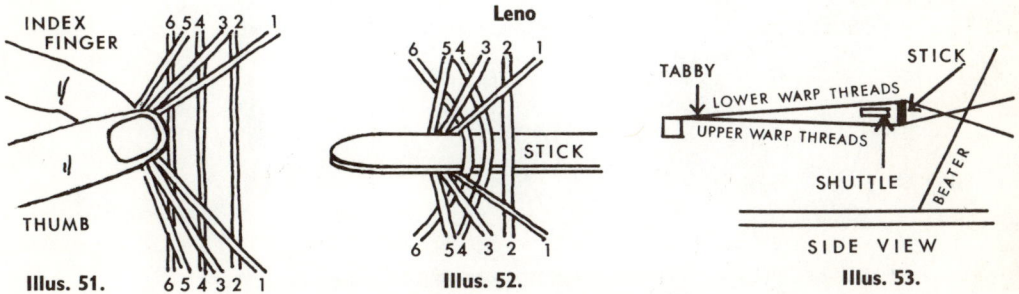

Illus. 51.

Leno

Illus. 52.

Illus. 53.

Illus. 54.
Leno
weave.

Beat hard before changing the shed. Then change the shed and beat very hard. Throw the shuttle from left to right and beat again.

When working on leno, work close to the tabby already woven in order to keep the last shot of tabby from loosening too much. Be sure to check often as you proceed across the row to see that all twists are alike.

Once you have learned leno, try making a place mat. Rough out a design on paper which will show the placement of the leno lines.

For a finer weave, you might try 2 over 2, instead of 3 over 3, or combine them in one mat or towel.

USE OF UNUSUAL MATERIALS

Strips of split bamboo, raffia, cattails, or other natural materials make striking table mats for informal settings. In this method of weaving, the warp, which is usually formed of heavy string, becomes the length of the mat (Illus. 55). You can combine natural materials with scraps of cloth, too, for unusual effects. The standard size for informal place mats is 12″ × 18″, but you can adjust the size to fit your table.

Since you will rarely want to weave just one place mat, when you calculate the warp, multiply the length of one place mat by as many as you want to make. Add to this figure a 6″ distance between each mat, plus a 36″ loom allowance. In this way you will be able to use the same warp without having to change it or make a new one for each separate mat. To separate the mats, weave several rows of candlewicking or rags between each one in the loom.

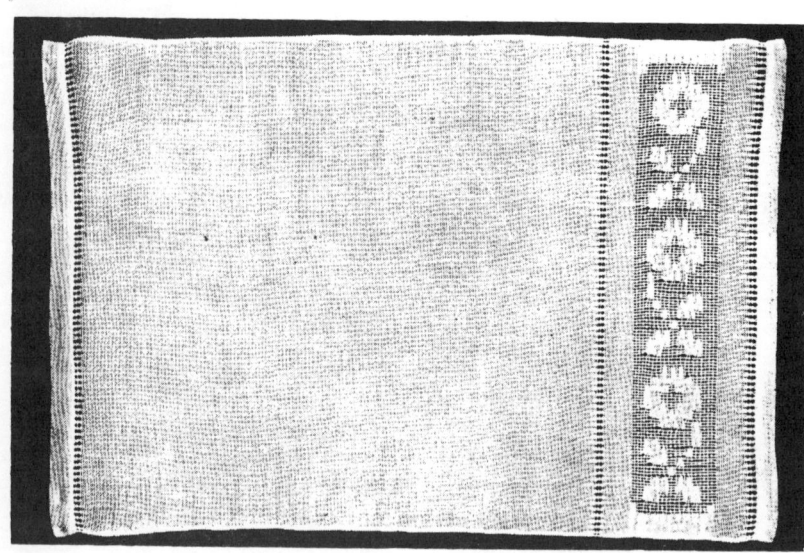

Illus. 55.
Leno
table
mat.

6. Weaving on a Four-Harness Loom

While you can weave many useful things on a two-harness loom, even as a beginner you will probably prefer a four-harness loom if you want to weave a variety of patterns and articles. Additional harnesses provide an infinite variety of possible combinations for the patterns which makes weaving such an interesting and rewarding hobby. Instead of being restricted to the tabby weave, which permits only those variations which can be achieved with colors (i.e. stripes and checks) and textures (ribs), you can vary the combinations of harnesses to make almost any designs your imagination can devise.

Even with a four-harness loom threaded for a plain tabby weave, by pressing down harness 1, then harness 2, then 3, and then 4, you can create a simple twill weave. Combinations—harnesses 1 and 2, 2 and 3, 3 and 4, or 1 and 3, 1 and 4—will produce basket weaves, random patterns, or anything you choose. It all depends on which harnesses you press down in what order. All weaving books and magazines have guides which tell you exactly how this is done for each pattern.

DRAFTS

If you can follow a recipe, you can follow *pattern drafts*, or guides. Once you master

drafts, there is practically no weaving pattern you cannot reproduce, and no pattern you cannot design, draft and execute yourself. Many beginning weavers are confused at first by drafts, since so many different methods are used to reproduce them, but once you know that all drafts, no matter how they are executed, give you the following information, you will not be confused:

1. The *threading draft* shows you how to thread the warp ends through the harnesses (i.e., which warp end goes through which harness in which heddle).

2. The *treadling draft* tells you which harnesses to press down in what order.

Illus. 56. Plain weave.

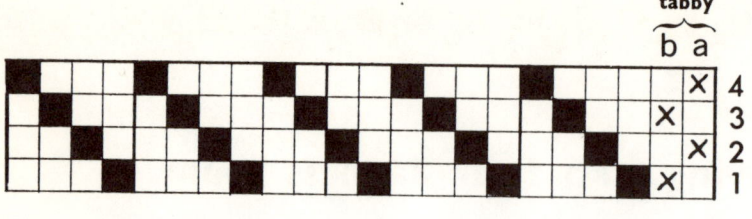

Illus. 57. Threading draft for plain weave in Illus. 56.

Illus. 58. Treadling draft for the left-hand twill in Illus. 59.

Threading Drafts

You already have some experience in working with *profile drafts* for the square weaver. Those profile drafts were planned on graph paper, and showed you how your finished design would look.

Illus. 57 is the *threading draft* for Illus. 56. It tells you to thread (from the right side of the loom to the left, as usual) the first warp end in the first heddle of harness 1, the second warp end through a heddle on harness 2 to the *left* of the first end on harness 1, the third end on harness 3, and the fourth on harness 4. Then, as the draft indicates, the fifth end is threaded on harness 1, as always in a heddle to the *left*

of the previous warp end. The sixth end is threaded through harness 2, the seventh on harness 3, the eighth on harness 4.

The last four ends have repeated what was done with the first four, and this is called a *pattern repeat.* Thus you would repeat this sequence across the entire warp to the width you desire for your project. All weaving drafts give the threading pattern only once or twice, and it is up to you to determine how many times you want to repeat it. The only exceptions are projects such as samplers or handbags which obviously have a limited pattern, and directions for these are usually given in full.

Treadling Drafts

Illus. 58 gives you the treadling instructions for Illus. 59 and is called a *treadling draft.* Also executed on graph paper and read from top to bottom, the numbers in the squares correspond to the harnesses on your loom. The first instruction in the lower right-hand corner

Illus. 59. Draft pattern for a left-hand twill.

Illus. 60. Treadling draft for tabby.

is "1", which refers to treadle 1, tied to harness 1. It means that for the first row of weaving that treadle should be depressed. As you can see by looking back to the pattern graph and threading draft, harness 1 will depress every fourth thread to form the first shed. Treadle 2 will operate harness 2 in the same way, depressing every fourth thread to the *left* of those lifted on harness 1.

Three and four work the same way, and by repeating this pattern over again (as with threading drafts the treadling draft is given only once, and you repeat it as often as necessary to complete the woven article) you will be forming a left-hand twill. By reversing the treadling, *without changing the threading*, you can weave a right-hand twill. Actually twills are more commonly woven double (that is, two ends each way) for sturdiness, but for our present purposes the single twill is more satisfactory since it enables you to understand the translation of draft-to-loom clearly.

Until you are more familiar with working with drafts you may want to experiment a bit at the loom. The threading draft you have just learned is actually the most basic one for the four-harness loom, and with this threading plan you can make many weaving patterns, just by varying the *treadling* patterns. For example,

let us suppose that the treadling directions were those shown in Illus. 60, which tells you to treadle 1 and 3 *together*, and then 2 and 4 together. The result would be the tabby weave, since every other thread would be lifted for each shed. Try various combinations on your loom (1 and 2, 3 and 4, then perhaps 1 and 4), repeating each several times. Then try to plot out what you have done on graph paper until you are comfortable with the feeling of "translating" drafts.

As you can see in Illus. 61, which is the same threading draft written in three different ways, it obviously doesn't matter whether the instructions are indicated in numbers, letters, or Chinese, as long as you understand them. With the above information, you should now be able to do so easily.

HOW TO INCORPORATE THE TABBY IN PATTERN WEAVING

The tabby weave engages every other thread in any given row, so it provides a "firm" weave no matter what the weaving material is. However, some patterns call for "long floats," in which the weft is carried over three or more warp threads before it is interlaced. If many pattern rows such as this occur together, you may have loops of yarn which might catch on

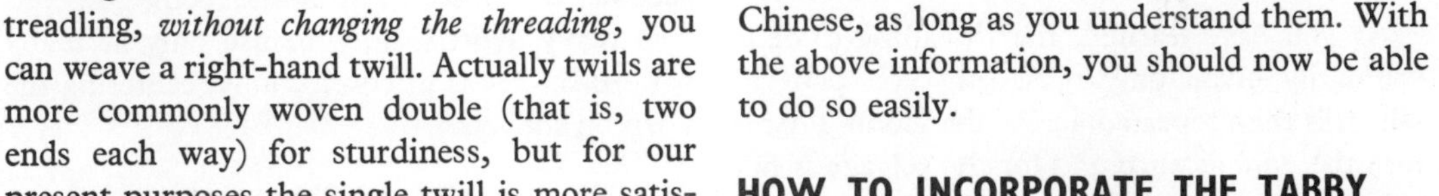

Illus. 61. Three ways of writing a threading draft.

other objects if the woven material were used for a dress or upholstery. Thus, some patterns require that you weave a row of tabby in between each pattern row, to anchor the design. If you like, you can use a lighter-weight weft thread (one which matches the warp) for the tabby. While the pattern will still be anchored, the tabby will be hardly visible. On the other hand, you may use the same weft for the tabby if it does not interfere with the design. The choice of using a tabby row in between each pattern row is up to you. In a tapestry, "floating" threads don't matter. Some designs have tightly knit patterns which would make a tabby superfluous. As you go along you will have to use your own judgment as to whether a particular pattern will need an anchoring tabby, since most drafts do not give this information.

SELVAGES AND DRAFTS

As you have learned, the threading draft is ordinarily given only once for each pattern, which is then repeated across the loom. Therefore the double warp end for the selvage is not usually indicated, since it would seem as though the intention were to indicate that every fourth heddle should be threaded double. It is left up to you in most cases to thread the first and last heddles double, but some drafts include selvage directions when they form special border arrangements that are threaded only at the beginning and the end. The selvage blocks are usually slightly shaded so that they can be distinguished from the pattern.

ESTIMATING THE WARP ENDS

Each draft shows a complete pattern. The number of *repeats* will depend upon the width of the article you want to weave, and the width of your loom. If one pattern has 75 threads, for

example, and you want three repeats, you will need 225 threads, plus two extra at each end for the selvage.

If you want to make something as wide as your loom, and your pattern would not come out evenly, you can solve the dilemma this way: Figure out how many blocks, including the selvages, you can possible have. Then count how many vacant dents this will leave in your reed. If you can make a 30″ strip on your loom, 15 dents to the inch, you will have to fill 450 dents. Let us suppose that you could use eight pattern blocks which require 50 threads each; allowing eight threads for selvage, you would have 42 empty dents. You could add to the design six groups of seven extra threads each between every two pattern blocks, threading them 1, 2, 3, 4, 3, 2, 1. This would give you your maximum width. Unless you absolutely *must* use the entire width of the loom, however, it is really a better idea to use only as many pattern blocks as fit comfortably, centering the warp on the loom.

THREADING THE LOOM

Before you begin, be sure to review the directions given in Chapter Three for dressing the loom. You should now be able to follow designs in the threading easily, but here are a few additional hints which will serve you well:

1. Be sure to tack your threading draft on to the harness brace of your loom, for you will be referring to it constantly. Until you become so expert that a look at your weaving will tell you where you are and what to do next, if you are called away from your task, stick a pin in the last square where you stop threading, so that you won't make a mistake when you come back to your work.

2. A thread in an even-numbered harness

must *always* be followed by one in an odd-numbered harness. For example, a thread on harness 1 must always be followed by a thread on either harness 2 *or* harness 4, while a thread on harness 2 must always be followed by one on either harness 1 or harness 3. If you have made a mistake in the threading, it need not be a fatal or final mistake. You *can* change the thread to its correct position by adding a new string heddle made of No. 12 seine cord. Be certain that you form and place each string heddle correctly so that its eye will be aligned with the standard metal heddles which come with the loom.

THE TIE-UP

A weaver's complete draft shows the threading pattern, the selvage, the tie-up, and the treadling.

Jack-type four-harness looms do not require a *tie-up*, because the harnesses are directly connected with the treadles by means of steel rods or chains, and there are no *lams*. The same is true for a table loom. Harness 1 is already permanently connected to treadle 1, harness 2 with treadle 2, and so on. These are *rising shed* looms, and they have only four treadles or levers. When a pattern calls for three treadles to be depressed at once, you must use one foot to depress two adjacent treadles and the other foot to depress the third treadle.

On counterbalanced looms, however, it is possible to depress two harnesses at once with one foot. This is because the lams, which resemble extending arms and hang midway between the harnesses and treadles, permit you to tie more than one harness to a treadle. By tying the harnesses to the lams and tying the lams to the treadles, you can obtain six

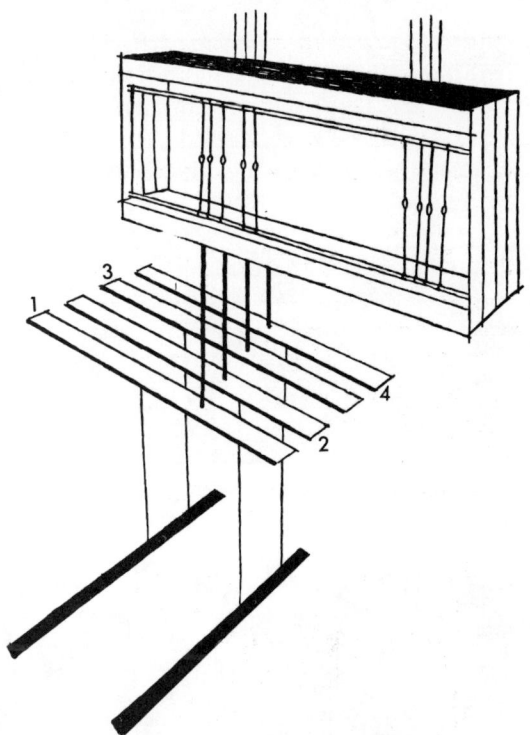

Illus. 62. The tie-up of a 4-harness loom.

different sheds on a four-harness loom. This, as you know, is most convenient when you plan to weave tabby rows between pattern rows.

Although we have suggested that you keep treadles 5 and 6 for your tabby, this is a purely arbitrary choice. Some weavers prefer to keep the two outside treadles for the tabby, some the two end ones, either right or left. The choice is up to you, as long as you remember that the other four treadles must be "re-numbered" 1 through to 4 if you do not use the last two for the tabby. This is because it might be confusing to you at first to remember that when the treadling draft indicates "1," it means the first *pattern* treadle.

51

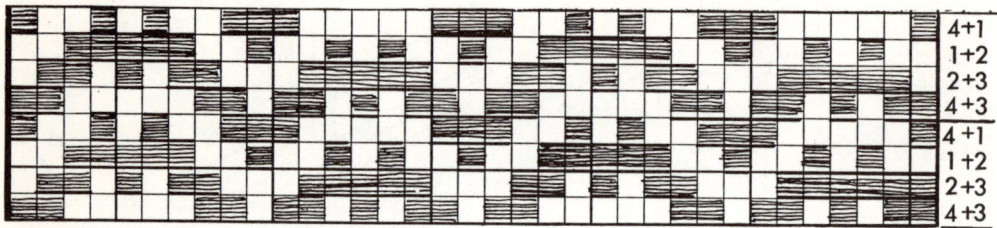

Illus. 63. Honeysuckle design, threading draft.

4+1
1+2
2+3
4+3
4+1
1+2
2+3
4+3

Illus. 64. Honeysuckle design, treadling.

1+2
2+3
3+4
1+4
3+4
2+3
1+2

1+3
2+4 } tabby

Illus. 65. Honeysuckle design, treadling draft variation with tabby.

Drafts drawn for a Jack-type loom use the letter "o" instead of "x" to indicate harnesses, so that you can distinguish at a glance whether a pattern is written for a Jack-type or counterbalanced loom.

TREADLING THE HONEYSUCKLE PATTERN

Illus. 63 is the threading draft for the Honeysuckle pattern, a simple and attractive design for small weaving. After you have copied the draft on graph paper, write the treadling directions underneath and tack them up on your loom: 4-1; 1-2; 2-3; 4-3. This means that first you depress treadles 4 and 1 together, and put in a shot of weft. Since this was a pattern shed, you must next put in a shot of tabby, which is not indicated on the treadling draft. Remember your tabby sheds are first 1-3, and then 2-4. So that there will be no mistake about inserting the tabby, you might revise the treadling directions to read:

4–1

1–2   one time each with tabby in

2–3   between.

4–3

Begin by weaving in a few rows of candle-wicking or rags to straighten out the warp, and then add an inch or two of tabby weave. Before you begin to weave the pattern, remember always to read and begin weaving from right to left, and beat each shot of weft in place as you go along.

If you want to add two or more different colors to the pattern, you will need a shuttle for each color as you did in Chapter Four. In order to keep the color sequence clear, you could add the following information to your treadling draft:

Blue 4–1

Gold 1–2   one time each, repeat

Gold 2–3

Blue 4–3

For a variation, you may use two or three shots of weft in each shed with a tabby binder between the pattern threads. Your treadling draft would then look like this:

Blue 4–1

Gold 1–2   3 times each, with tabby in

Gold 2–3   between, repeat

Blue 4–3

You have now learned all the basic principles of weaving on a four-harness loom, which is not much different from weaving on eight-, twelve-, or even 16-harness looms. From now on your only limitation will be your imagination. There are hundreds of thousands of weaving patterns in books and magazines on your library shelves, none of which will be too difficult for you now—if you are patient. In the next chapter we will introduce you to a few of the interesting patterns available.

7. How to Weave Patterns on a Four-Harness Loom

Now that you know the important principles involved in weaving on a four-harness loom, you are ready to design and complete your first weaving project. We like to think this chapter will not only "open doors" to a world of beautiful weaves, but also provide you with many happy hours at the loom and a profitable hobby. A weaver can find hundreds of four-harness patterns already worked out in good weaving books and other publications. You will find that each book or publication may have a different system of indicating patterns and other directions, but all have the same underlying principles we have described in this book. For this reason, we want to give further interpretation to some of the familiar patterns in the field of weaves.

We will not try in a single chapter to discuss all the possibilities and variations of four-harness patterns, but we have chosen three basic weaves that every weaver will use over and over because of their versatility as well as beauty:

1. *Twills*. First of all, we have chosen twills because the different patterns are produced with the simplest succession of harnesses it is possible to thread on a four-harness loom. In the twill itself the weft usually passes over and under two warp threads at a time, and never more than three. For this reason, only one weft thread is required and the weaving goes very rapidly.

2. *Over-Shot Weaves*. Over-shot patterns consist of large blocks of groups of threads in a different weight and color with the appearance of being superimposed on a plain background. This is the most versatile of all weaves because many different designs can be produced from variations in the treadling of a single threading on the harnesses. Another important principle involved is the use of a tabby thread for binding in the over-shot patterns. This type of weaving is done with two shuttles, one of which carries the fine tabby thread, the other, the coarse pattern thread.

3. *Dukägang*. The pillarlike motifs in this weave add touches of bright colors to useful and decorative fabrics such as those used for household linens and borders on dress materials. Another reason for selecting this weave is to explain the use of a "Weaving Sword" for laying-in patterns on a two-harness loom.

TWILLS

One has only to examine commercially-woven fabrics in a department store to realize

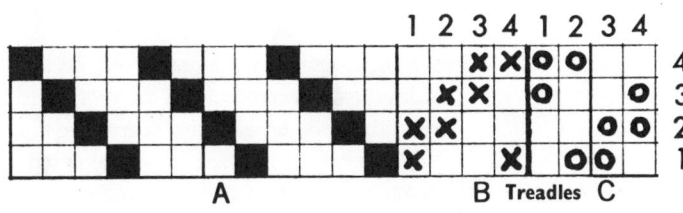

**Illus. 66.
Dukagäng
weave.**

the popularity of twills in the field of weaves. Most of the clothes we wear are woven with some variations of twill—plain twill, cheveron, or checks, just to mention a few. Contrasting colors of warp and weft produce interesting fabrics such as the Scottish tartans and Irish tweeds. Many fine linens are also woven in twill. No attempt will be made to present all the possibilities of twill threadings or treadling, but we will try to explain the system upon which this weave is based.

The standard threading for twill is the same as for plain weave, Illus. 67 (A), but the tie-up is different. The tie-up for a counterbalanced loom is indicated by "x's" in the B section of the draft and by "o's" in the C section for the Jack loom. Instead of weaving alternately on harnesses 1–3 and 2–4 as in plain weave, one

**Illus. 67.
Standard
threading
for twill.**

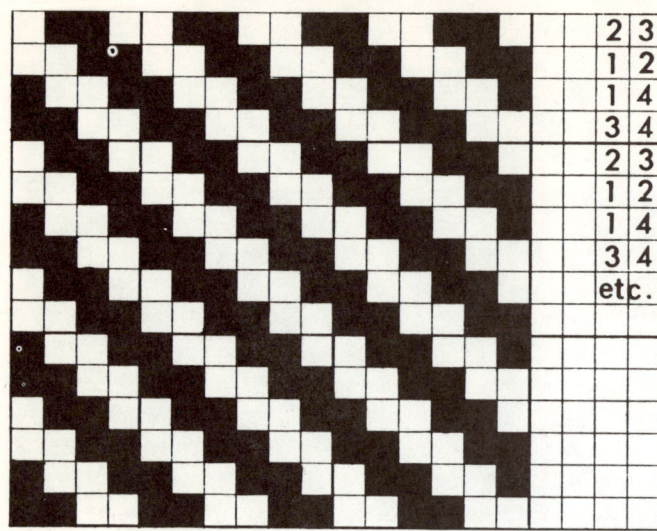

Illus. 68. Treadling draft for a left-hand twill.

Illus. 69. Treadling draft for a right-hand twill.

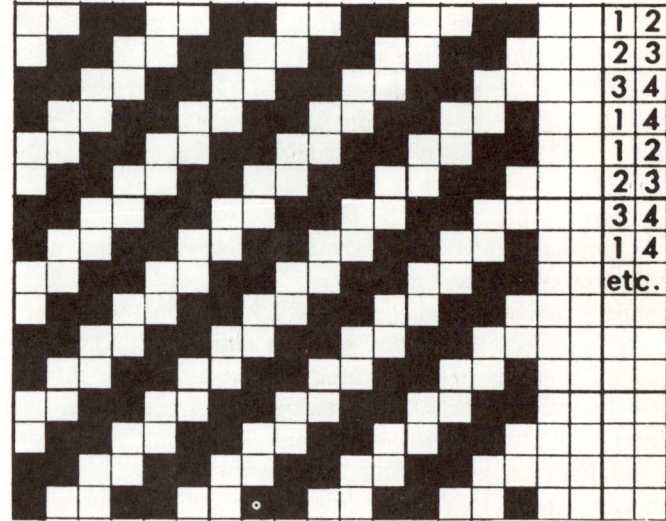

uses adjacent harnesses 1–2, 2–3, 3–4 and 4–1 in succession. Since the weft goes over and under only two or three warp threads at a time, there is no need for tabby to bind the rows together.

Twill patterns can be changed by using different tie-ups, changing sequence of threading, or adding color variations in the warp and weft. The slightest change in threading or treadling produces a different result. If the pattern progresses a single thread to the right or left, the result is either a right-hand or left-hand twill.

In weaving a simple four-harness twill pattern, the first shot passes *over* all warp threads threaded on harnesses 1–2 and *under* all on 3–4. The second shot passes *over* all warp threads threaded on harnesses 2–3 and *under* all on 1–4. The third shot passes *over* all warp threads on harnesses 3–4 and *under* all on 1–2. The fourth shot passes *over* all warp threads threaded on harnesses 4–1 and *under* all on 2–3.

Left-Hand Twill (Illus. 68)

A continued repetition of 2–3, 1–2, 1–4, 3–4 sequence produces a left-hand twill.

Right-Hand Twill (Illus. 69)

The reversal of the above sequence 1–2, 2–3, 3–4, 1–4 produces a right-hand twill.

One-and-Three Twill (Illus. 70)

This twill weave produces a fabric showing more warp on one side and more weft on the opposite side. The treadling is as follows:

Use harness 1 alone, 2 alone, 3 alone and 4 alone and repeat. When each single harness is lowered, the other three are raised and more warp shows on the surface. To obtain the opposite effect with more weft showing on the surface, weave by pressing three harnesses at a

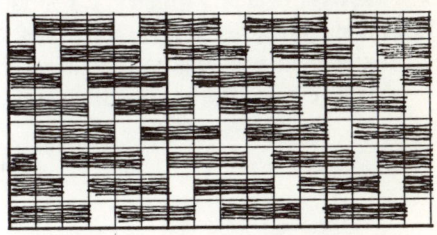

Illus. 70. Drafts for one-and-three twill.

time; weave 1, 2 and 3 together, then weave 2, 3 and 4, harnesses 3, 4 and 1, and harnesses 4, 1 and 2, and repeat.

Zigzag Twill (Illus. 71)

The zigzag effect is produced by first repeating the treadling for a left-hand twill and then treadling for the right-hand twill.

Illus. 71. Zigzag twill.

Point Twill (Illus. 72)

Many of the important twill patterns are the result of variations in threading the four harnesses. To produce horizontal zigzag effects, the pattern must be threaded through the different harnesses so it can be reversed at threading points in the heddles. One can reverse on any thread in plain twill, either in the middle of a repeat, or at the end of a repeat. Point twill effects are produced by reversing the pattern at the threading point so that a single thread appears at the top of the triangle.

Illus. 72 shows a draft in which the reverse takes place on the *fifth* thread (A). This causes a reverse in the twill weaving at the point at which there is a reverse on the treadling draft.

Weave
   1–2
   2–3
   3–4
   4–1
Reverse at this point to
   3–4   2–3 and repeat 1–2, etc.

Illus. 73. Herringbone pattern.

Herringbone Patterns

The herringbone, with its diagonals going first in one direction and then in another, is a popular pattern when it comes to weaving fabrics for suiting, upholstery, draperies and even for household linens. The width of each stripe or unit is governed by the number of

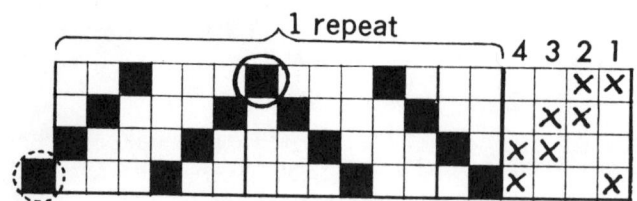

Illus. 74. Threading draft for a herringbone twill. The circled thread is only threaded at the end.

Illus. 75. Different herringbone draft of 28 threads. Treadling is the same, however.

threads used in each repeat. There may be two, three or more repeats of regular twill successions before reversing at the turning point.

Illus. 74 is a threading draft for a simple herringbone pattern showing a two-twill succession of four rows each and then a reverse at "A" with the same number. Illus. 75 shows a draft that has 28 threads to complete the unit.

Treadling
    1–2
    2–3
    3–4
    4–1   Repeat as often as necessary

Broken Twills (Herringbone) (Illus. 76 and 77)

Repeating four or more rows of plain twill and then reversing the treadling the same number of times will produce a fabric with its diagonals going first in one direction and then in another. The result will be a herringbone pattern as shown in Illus. 76:

If you study the patterns carefully in Illus. 76 and 77, you will see that there is a double row of black squares where the reversing takes place instead of a continuous line as shown in Illus. 73. Herringbone is always a broken twill

Illus. 76. Broken twill pattern with its threading draft.

pattern but a broken twill is not always herringbone. This brings us to another principle involved in weaving twills.

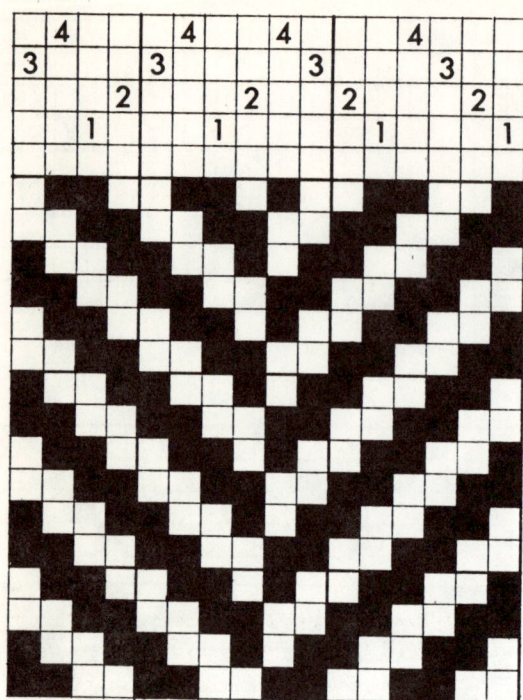

Illus. 77. Another broken twill with its threading draft.

Broken Twill Originals

Many weavers try to accomplish something creative at the loom. Today, with so many new and exciting yarns on the market, color as well as texture in the warp and weft play an increasingly important part in our weaving designs. Broken twill patterns, where the threadings may follow a succession of colors regardless of the number of heddles in the unit, give a decided modern and new appearance to finished material. Any number of colors may be employed in the warping plan as long as they are repeated throughout the width of the fabric.

Let's say you have chosen three colors for your design—Medium Blue, Turquoise and Light Blue:

Warping Plan

(1) Two ends of Medium Blue

(2) Two ends of Turquoise

(3) One end of Light Blue

The sett would be:

One Medium Blue in heddles 1 and 2

One Turquoise in heddles 3 and 4

One Light Blue in heddle 5, which is the second heddle on the first harness.

Tie-Up

Use standard tie-up for weaving twills.

Goose-Eye Pattern

This pattern, as shown in the draft (Illus. 79), is woven with three twill successions followed by a reverse. If woven as drawn in,

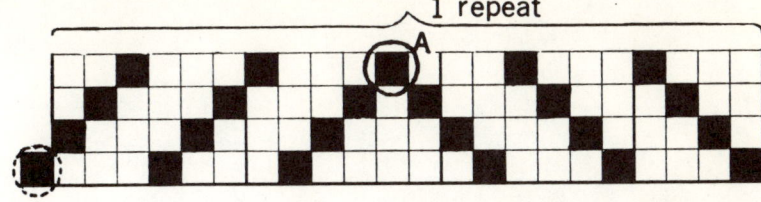

Illus. 78. Threading draft for goose-eye pattern. The circled thread is only threaded at the end.

the result will be an enclosed diamond known as the Goose-Eye. In order to bring out the diamond effect, follow the harnesses in groups of two as they come in the threading draft reading from right to left. Weave as follows:

1–2
2–3
3–4
4–1
1–2
2–3

Reverse at this point to

1–2
4–1
3–4
2–3 and repeat all

WEAVING WITH THREE SHUTTLES

Start the first yarn color shuttle from the right side of the loom; the second yarn color shuttle from the opposite side of the loom (left); and the third shuttle from the same side of the loom from which the first shuttle was started. Having done this, you will find the correct colored yarn shuttle waiting to be used after a shot of weft is thrown through a particular shed. This procedure saves the weaver much confusion regarding what shuttle is next in the weft-shot sequence. If, at any time, you find that you have three shuttles on the same

Illus. 79. Goose-eye pattern—an enclosed diamond.

side of the loom, you can be assured that you have made a mistake in your weft order.

WOOLLEN FABRICS

The fabrics shown in Illus. 80 were designed by the Countryside Handweavers to show

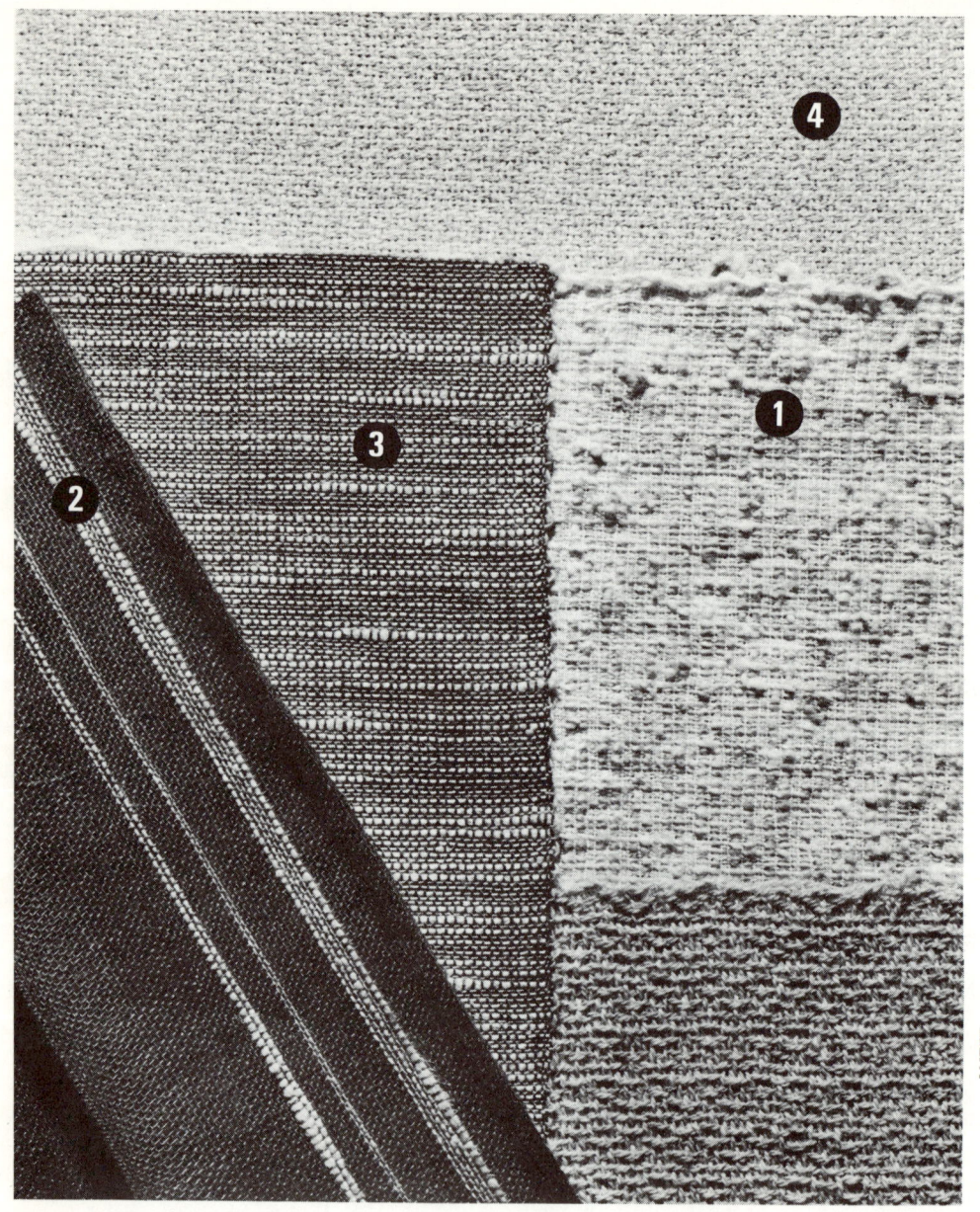

WEFT ⟶

Illus. 80. Broken twills.

											1	2	3	4	a	b		Harness
O			O			O			M			O				X	X			X	4
	M			M			M			M			M		X	X			X		3
		O			M			O			O			M		X	X			X		2
		M			M			M			M			M		X			X	X		1

Illus. 81. Threading draft for nubby twill, (1) in Illus. 80.

surface interest from their imported Swiss yarns. The drafts (Illus. 81 and Illus. 82) are typical of ones used to indicate that a number of different textures, yarns, or colors are used in a design. Here, letters are used instead of squares to indicate warp ends—a system that is most helpful when it comes to threading the heddles.

In the above threading for a nubby twill, (1) in Illus. 80, "O" indicates nubby wool and nylon and "M" mohair and wool. Use the standard tie-up at the right of the draft in Illus. 81.

Treadling: Starting with mohair and wool, treadle three times with harnesses 1—3, followed by 2—4, then 1—3. Then with nubby wool, treadle 2—4. Then 1 shot of mohair and wool on 1—2, followed by 1 shot of nubby wool on 2—4, then repeat.

The napkin shown as (2) in Illus. 80 is woven of black linen with varying stripes of orange and tangerine for a border. The place mat (3) in Illus. 80 has a hem of $\frac{3}{4}''$ of black liners for turn under.

No. 4 in Illus. 80 is a broken twill with a two-ply woollen warp consisting of three colors: lemon yellow (L), yellow green (Y), and gold (G). The threading and tie-up are shown in Illus. 82.

Treadle 4, 3, 2, 1. Repeat.

OVER-SHOT PATTERNS

Over-shot patterns are made up of blocks of warp threads in a contrasting color or texture which are superimposed on a plain woven background. If the design threads were cut away, the tabby web would remain. The pattern yarn spans or skips over a certain number of warp ends as it is guided through the shed, and each row is followed by a tabby thread running in the opposite direction. Two shuttles are needed—one for tabby, the other for pattern or heavier thread. (See Illus. 83, page 64). The pattern threads are packed or beaten so closely during the weaving process that the web is almost covered.

Practically all over-shot patterns are drafted in such a manner that harnesses 1–3, 2–4 are

Selvage

	G		G			L		L			Y		Y			X		X	4
	Y			L		G			Y	G	L			G		Y		X	X	3
L		L		Y		Y				Y	G				G		X	X		2
	G			Y			L		G				L		L		X	X		1

Illus. 82. Threading pattern for broken twill, (4) in Illus. 80.

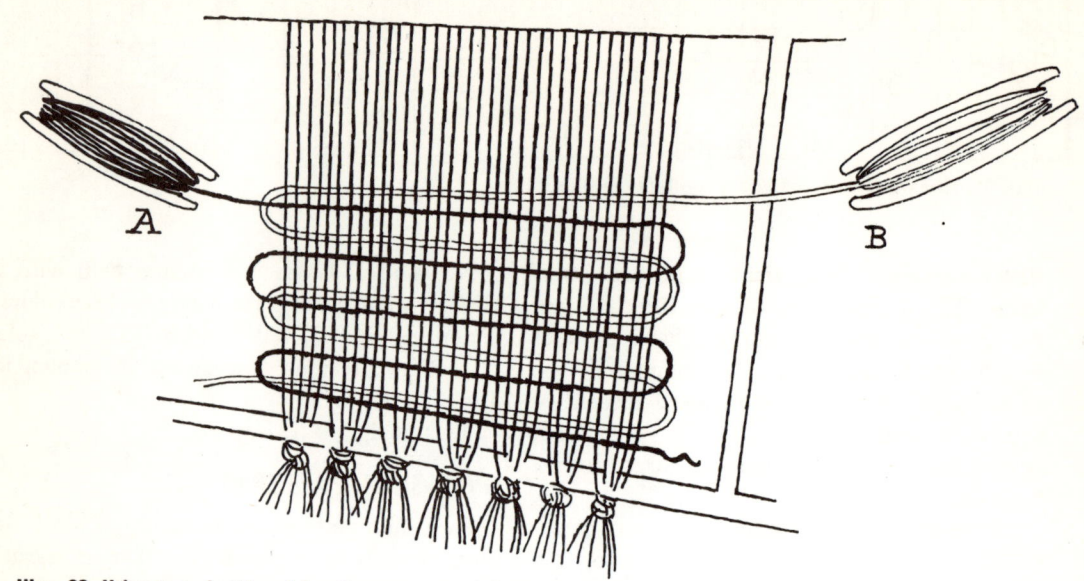

Illus. 83. Using two shuttles, A for the pattern or heavier thread, B for the tabby.

used for tabby weave, leaving the four combinations 1–2, 2–3, 3–4, 4–1 for the pattern shots. Since it is taken for granted that the weaver will alternate the pattern rows with tabby regularly, tabby notations are omitted from the treadling directions.

Variation in the pattern is obtained by the number of repeats in a pattern block. For instance, if a very heavy pattern weft thread is used, the blocks will build up very quickly and fewer repeats will be required. The weaver is at liberty to weave the blocks fewer or more times in order to make each block square in the pattern.

While there are the over-all characteristics of over-shot weaving, each pattern will be somewhat different. Let us consider several familiar patterns and continue our analysis.

Honeysuckle Pattern (Illus. 63)

Honeysuckle has more variations than any other over-shot pattern because of the small motif in the design. Hundreds of combinations may be woven with one threading so this is an excellent choice for a novice who has never done pattern weaving on a four-harness loom. In fact, it would be an excellent idea to weave a sampler or wall hanging showing rows of the different variations. These can be used later on for border designs or an all-over pattern. The use of different colored and textured thread for the weft will also help the weaver understand the relation between the tabby web and pattern threads. Separate the pattern rows with several rows of plain weave and be sure to keep a record for each treadling sequence for reference later on.

Dukagäng table mats.

Over-shot pattern.

Dukagäng pattern with vertical stripes.

Monk's Belt pattern.

Monk's Belt Pattern

The Monk's Belt pattern is made up of small motifs resembling crosses set between woven squares. The arrangement of these crosses may be altered at will and you can find innumerable threading drafts for this pattern but all will have one principle in common:

The Monk's Belt belongs to the family of Patch Patterns which are composed of contrasting motifs of square blocks said to be "on opposite." This means that one square is threaded on opposite harnesses 1 and 2, while the other is threaded on harnesses 3 and 4. Harness combinations 2–3 and 1–4 are not needed to produce a simple two-block pattern. The size of the blocks may be changed by increasing or decreasing the number of threads in each block.

Band in Monk's Belt (Color plate opposite)

This is a two-block pattern which has only two treadling combinations to produce the squares—1 and 2, 2 and 4; alternating with tabby, of course. The treadling would be written:

Tabby
  1–3 left
  2–4 right
Pattern
  1–2–5x
  3–4–5x

Note that the first block of the pattern (No. 1 on the draft) consists of a number of 1's and 2's (harnesses) threaded in sequence; therefore treadles 1 and 2 are used to open the shed for the insertion of the shuttle which carries the pattern thread for the first block of the pattern. This treadling (alternating with tabby) will continue until enough pattern threads are woven to form a square, which in this case is five. In block No. 2 of the pattern draft the square is threaded on harnesses 3 and 4. Treadle this block until another block

**Illus. 84.
Mat with
Monk's Belt
pattern.**

Illus. 85. Small over-shot Monk's Belt band.

has been woven. Return to the treadling of the first block, and so on, until the desired length has been woven.

To weave the orange and black columns in the green mat (color plate), treadle one block only with tabby thread between. The sequence in the pattern would be

Black 1–2 × 3
Orange 1–2 × 14
Black 1–2 × 3

Small Over-shot Pattern

Illus. 85–86–87 are included because small units from over-shot patterns can be used separately to form borders or small designs scattered over a plain web.

1)	1	+	2	
	1	+	3	X
2)	1	+	2	
	2	+	4	X
3)	1	+	2	
	1	+	3	X
4)	1	+	2	
	2	+	4	X
5)	1	+	2	
	1	+	3	X
1)	3	+	4	
	2	+	4	X
2)	3	+	4	
	1	+	3	X
3)	3	+	4	
	2	+	4	X
4)	3	+	4	
	1	+	3	X
5)	3	+	4	
	2	+	4	X
Repeat				
X	=	tabby		

Illus. 86. Treadling sequence for band in Monk's Belt. For each block the pattern thread is thrown 5 times, alternating with tabby weave. The pattern blocks are 1+2 and 3+4. Tabby is 1+3 and 2+4.

66

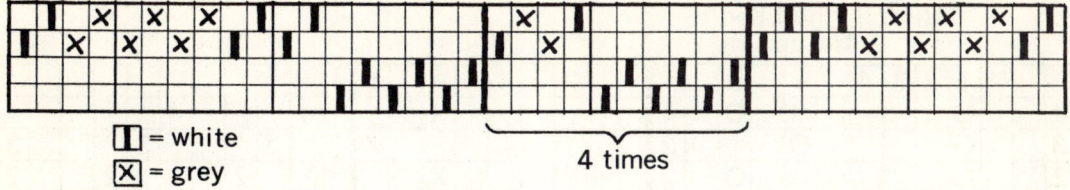

☐ = white
☒ = grey

4 times

Illus. 87. Weaving draft for small over-shot band in Monk's Belt.

This draft also has a treadling system used by many weavers internationally. (See Illus. 86.) Each horizontal row in the treadling draft represents one row of weaving and the No. 1 indicates the harnesses that are to be lowered or raised. In this pattern, harnesses 1–3 are lowered in the first row, 2–4 the second, and so on.

(In foreign drafts the harnesses are often numbered back to front, so that No. 4 would be the one nearest you.)

DUKAGÄNG

For a 2-harness loom, you can use a "Weaving Sword"; however, for dukagäng on a 4-harness loom, this is not necessary.

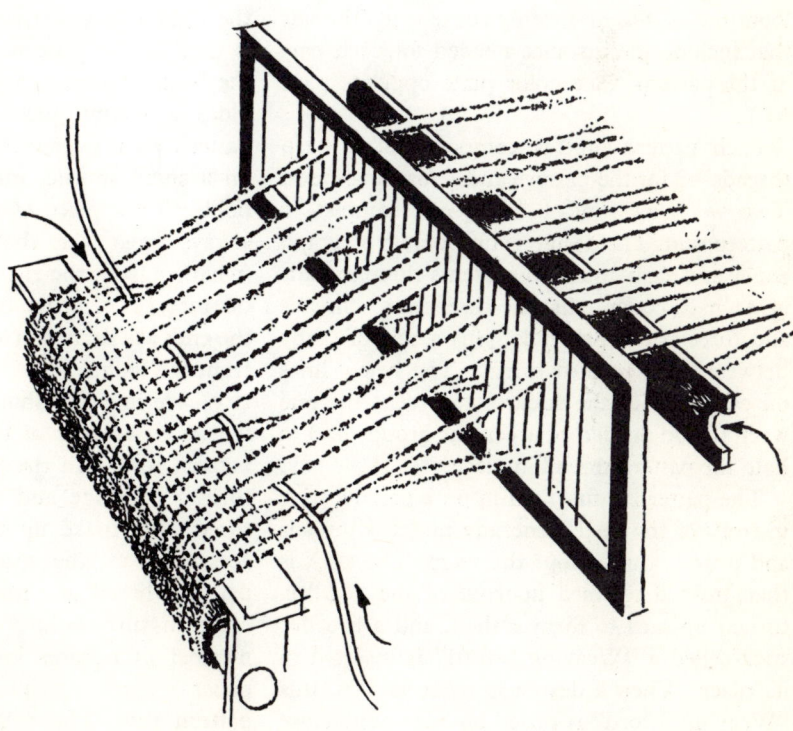

Illus. 88. A "Weaving Sword." This has to be used in weaving Dukagäng on a 2-harness loom.

Rising Shed Loom

	tie-up							tie-up						threading					
	1	2	3	4	a	b		1	2	3	4	a	b						
4	O					O	4					X		4			4			4
3	O				O		3						X		3			3		3
2	O					O	2					X				2			2	2
1					O		1	X					X				1		1	1

Illus. 89. Threading draft for Dukagäng, a Swedish folk pattern.

Dukagäng is a design made up of vertical lines superimposed on a 50/50 tabby web. It is a Swedish folk art technique that is used by modern weavers to decorate wall hangings, initials on household linens and, more particularly, for borders on guest towels and place mats. The pattern thread in this type of weaving does not extend entirely across the loom but is woven on only those warp threads that include the distance needed for each part of the pattern. (See color plate opposite page 64.)

Each pattern unit is composed of 4 warp threads—3 for the pattern and 1 for the binder. Two weft rows and 1 tabby row complete a pattern unit. The design is first drawn on graph paper and each square represents three threads in each direction, that is, three warp threads and three pattern threads, plus a row of tabby between each pattern thread. The heavy lines on each side of the squares represent the one warp thread needed between the groups of 3 to hold the pattern thread in place.

The pattern is first laid in on a narrow stick in front of the reed, generally under 3 threads and over 1, throughout the warp. The stick is then pushed forward in front of the heddles, turned upward to form a shed, and a broader stick called a "Weaving Sword" is inserted in its place. When a design is to be laid-in, this "Weaving Sword" is raised on edge quite close to the heddles and one sees the shed that has come up quite close to the reed where the inlay is made.

When tabby shots are called for, the "Weaving Sword" has to be removed to permit treadling of the tabby shed.

Dukagäng designs are woven with the wrong side of the pattern up towards the weaver and the right side underneath unless a single color is used in the pattern. This method facilitates the beginning and ending of threads and provides a resting place for small bobbins of pattern yarn. Each color yarn should be wound on a small shuttle, into a ball, or as a small bobbin on a piece of paper. Each color must always enter the shed from the same side (whether from the right or from the left). The bobbins lie in order on the finished web and the ends are darned in after the cloth is removed from the loom.

Weave in a few shots of tabby, or a border, if it is to be part of the design. For the first pattern row, pull the "Sword Stick" forward, turn it on edge and count off the group of threes that make up the pattern in that row according to the graph design. Insert the pattern thread at these points and pass each color in turn *towards the right* covering the number of squares indicated on the squared paper. A row of plain tabby follows each pattern row. The pattern rows are repeated three times or until the unit has been squared up.

If you have a four-harness loom, the process of weaving in Dukagäng patterns is much simpler because the warp threads are manipulated by the treadles instead of the insertion of a "Weaving Sword." The loom is treadled on a four-harness twill and woven as indicated below.

Treadling

Weave a few rows of tabby, ending with a 2–4 tabby. On treadle 1 enter the pattern thread from the right.

Tabby from the right on 1 + 3.

Pattern on 1 from the left.

Tabby on 2 + 4 from the left.

Repeat until pattern has been completed.

Some weavers use two tabby shots between each pattern shot—this also depends on your yarn size.

These directions are for weaving the pattern on the underside of the web. If one color only is used, the pattern may be woven right side up. To do this, use the counterbalance treadling for the Jack loom and vice versa.

(*Note:* When designs are woven with wrong side of the pattern towards the weaver and the right side underneath, it sometimes makes it necessary to read the pattern from left to right. By holding the graph against a window so that the light shines through it the pattern can be retraced, thereby making it easier to follow while weaving.)

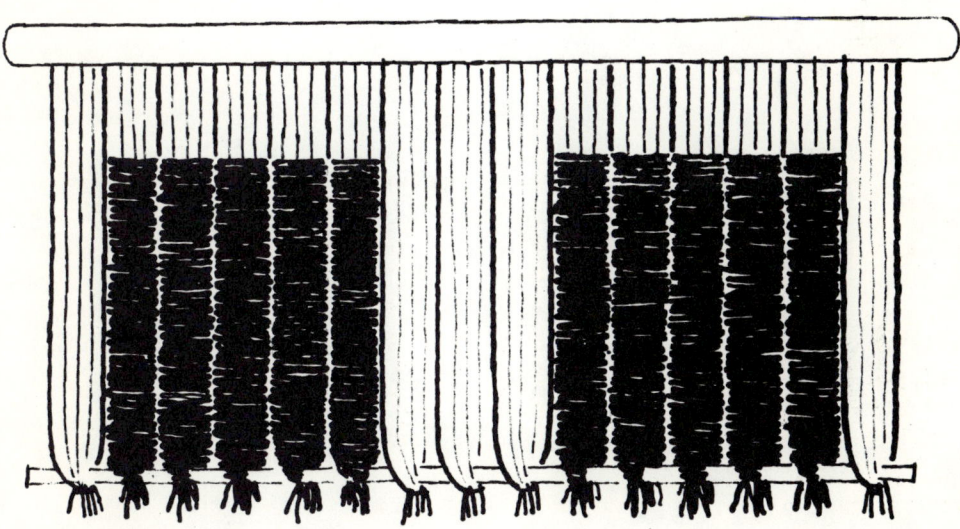

Illus. 90. Dukagäng pattern.

INDEX